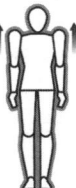

One Hundred Stretches

One Hundred Stretches

JimBrown

ILLUSTRATIONS BY MARTY BEE

BURFORD BOOKS

Printed in Canada.

10 9 8 7 6 5 4 3 2 1

Library of Congress Cataloging-in-Publication Data

Brown, Jim.
  One hundred stretches : a guide for athletes / Jim Brown.
     p. cm.
  ISBN 1-58080-125-0 (pbk.)
  1. Physical education and training. 2. Stretching exercises. I. Title: 100 stretches. II. Title.

  GV711.5.B78 2004
  613'.7'182—dc22

                              2004012948

DISCLAIMER *One Hundred Stretches* is not intended to give personal medical or training advice, which should be obtained directly from a physician, physical therapist, or other health care professional. Acting on any information provided in this book without first consulting a physician is solely at the reader's risk.

613.7182
BRO
2004

Contents

Introduction

Why stretch? To feel good and move with ease. Why one hundred stretches? To provide choices. Whether you are a world-class athlete, a dedicated exerciser, or someone beginning a program, choose stretches that are right for your body, your age, and your fitness level. Do them at home, at work, or in a gym—outside or inside. Carry this book as a reminder and pocket instructor.

Chapter 1 makes the case for stretching with seven compelling arguments. It also tells you what stretching won't do and when not to stretch. Chapter 2 helps you decide on the kind of stretches that are appropriate for you and warns you about ones that are potentially dangerous, and chapter 3 gives guidelines that make those stretches effective and safe.

Chapters 4, 5, 6, and 7 include one hundred descriptions and illustrations of stretches for the lower body, trunk, and upper body—from the toes to the fingers and everything in between. You can do them while sitting, standing, or lying, and you can perform stretches that involve light resistance.

Design your own stretching routine or use one of the sample programs in Chapters 8 and 9. There are sport-specific stretches for baseball/softball, basketball, football, golf, jogging/running, skiing, soccer, swimming, tennis, and volleyball. There are also "special situation" stretches for those starting a program, those sitting at desks all day or watching television or traveling in the confined spaces of cars and airplanes. There are even stretches for the places that hurt most often —the back, shoulders, and knees.

If either of us missed something in chapters 1 through 9, there are answers to twenty frequently asked questions in chapter 10.

I have tried all one hundred stretches to make sure they are sensible and useful—no weird contortions that require the flexibility of a circus performer. I work at a computer, travel occasionally, watch too many ball games on TV, and try to exercise every day. I also have a back that needs all the support it can get. *One Hundred Stretches* was written for you and for me. Hope it helps.

—Jim Brown

The Case for Stretching

S tretching is temporarily making muscles longer by using certain kinds of exercises. It gets credit for everything from feeling good, whatever that means, to running faster and jumping higher. Stretching is recommended and even prescribed by doctors, and it is widely practiced by exercisers and athletes in almost every sport. Whether you are a neighborhood walker or a competitive athlete, stretching just seems to be one of those common-sense things to do.

But if you are going to invest the time and effort to stretch, there are plenty of questions about stretching that require a closer look. Does it make the body's joints more flexible? Will it improve athletic performance? Can it help you prevent injuries? Does it have anything to do with balance? Does it improve circulation? Will it make you feel better? Can it delay the effects of aging? Following are the answers to those questions.

Become More Flexible

Does stretching make the body's joints more flexible? Yes. There is conclusive evidence regarding stretching and flexibility. Loss of flexibility can be prevented and at least partially restored by stretching. The evidence is more compelling for a long-term stretching program than for shorter periods of time. Stretching to increase flexibility minutes prior to an event might or might not work, but a stretching program over a period of months can lead to a sustained increase in range of motion.

Enhance Performance

Does stretching improve athletic performance? Yes, if the stretches are designed to be sport-specific—that is, they mimic the motions needed for that sport. One study showed that an increase in the temperature of a muscle in the upper leg achieved by stretching resulted in a higher vertical jump and added the power needed in cycling. But that study did not investigate whether or not the increase in temperature could have been achieved by other warm-up methods. Another study showed that a ten-week stretching program resulted in improved performance in speed, strength, power, and muscle endurance. Additional research has shown benefits in throwing a baseball and serving a tennis ball following a stretching program that improved shoulder flexibility. Finally, freer and easier movement enhances coordination, and people who play sports need great coordination to perform at a high level.

Prevent Injuries . . . . Maybe

Does stretching help prevent injuries? The supporting evidence is not as clear on this subject. The authors of a study reported in the Clinical Journal of Sport Medicine say, "New evidence suggests that stretching immediately before exercise does not prevent overuse or acute injuries." They added that continuous stretching during the day and conducted over a period of time might indeed promote muscle growth, which in turn could reduce the risk of injury.

There is another indirect connection between stretching and injuries. Stretching is known to increase range of motion, and exercisers who have less-than-ideal ROM are more susceptible to muscle and joint injuries.

Lyle Micheli, the well-known orthopedic surgeon and author from Boston, says in his *Sports Medicine Bible*, "Regular flexibility training prevents injuries such as muscle strains, ligament sprains, and shin splints." And the American Academy of Orthopaedic Surgeons, among other professional medical groups, recommends stretches to protect against certain sports-related injuries.

Stretching routines can provide several benefits. If injuries are prevented along the way, consider it a bonus. While the case for stretching to prevent injuries is not airtight, there is support from a wide range of medical experts and organizations. When stretching does not prevent injuries, it may have more to do with kinds of stretches, how they are conducted, and when they are performed than with the act of stretching itself.

Maintain Balance

Is there a connection between stretching and balance? Yes, says the Mayo Clinic. "Maintaining the full range of motion through your joints [by stretching] keeps you in better balance. Especially as you get older, coordination and balance will help keep you mobile and less prone to injury from falls."

Improve Circulation

Does stretching improve circulation? Yes, it does. Stretching and other warm-up activities increase the amount of blood that flows to the muscles. That blood flow brings nutrients with it and gets rid of waste products that have accumulated in muscle tissue. Improved circulation can help reduce the amount of time it takes to recover after an injury to a muscle. One of the first things a physical therapist does in a rehabilitation program is guide the patient through mild, passive stretching exercises.

Feel Better

Does stretching actually make you feel better? It should reduce stiffness and make you feel more relaxed. There is a program in this book designed for your age, body, and activity level that will positively affect the way you feel.

But don't take my word for it. Get started on a stretching program and decide for yourself. Odds are you'll feel better.

Delay the Effects of Aging

Fifty is not a magic number, but it represents the age at which people noticeably begin losing flexibility. It may happen sooner, maybe later. But it's going to happen unless you do something about it. You'll start noticing that it's harder to bend or twist. Your ability to easily swing a golf club, tennis racket, or any other piece of sports equipment will diminish. You may suffer nagging muscle strains or joint sprains more often than when you were younger. But all of this doesn't have to happen. There are ways to maintain or regain a full range of motion in all your joints. Those ways are included in a systematic program of stretching.

Ten Times Not to Stretch

Stretching is not for everybody. There are conditions and situations, most of them temporary, in which stretching could cause or complicate an existing medical problem. Below are ten of them. If you have any doubts or questions about the appropriateness of a stretching program, consult a physician who has a background in exercise, fitness, or sports medicine. Don't stretch . . . .

➤ if you have one or more involved joints that are not stable or overly lax.

➤ if you have certain vascular diseases.

➤ if you have had recent surgery.

➤ if you have suffered a recent muscle or tendon strain.

➤ if you have suffered a recent sprained (stretched, torn, or ruptured) ligament.

➤ if you have recently broken a bone.

➤ if you have osteoporosis.

➤ if you have acute pain upon movement.

➤ if there is inflammation or infection in the area of the involved joint.

> if you have been sedentary for a long period of time and have not consulted a physician about beginning a program.

What Stretching Won't Do

Stretching is not a complete exercise package. It might increase your rate of circulation, but it is not going to do anything for cardiovascular or cardiopulmonary fitness. For that to happen, the heart rate has to increase to a target level and stay there for a while. Stretching won't do it. A separate aerobic fitness program will.

The purpose of stretching is not to increase muscle strength or muscle endurance. There is some evidence that strength gains may occur with certain types of stretches, but consider those gains an added benefit. To get stronger, consider a resistance training routine. A complete exercise program includes stretching, aerobic fitness training, and resistance exercises.

Young Athletes and Stretching

There is surprisingly little evidence on the effects of stretching on young athletes and exercisers. There are those think stretching prevents injuries and enhances performance, but it's just not possible to document those beliefs at this point. Most of what has been written and said is based on opinion, anecdotal evidence, common sense, and in some cases, downright misconceptions rather than on scientific studies. Here is what we do know.

First of all, kids don't like to stretch. (Have you ever heard a child ask to be able to do more stretching?) And if they don't like it—if it's not fun—they probably won't do it. So the first suggestion for parents and youth coaches is not to make static stretching (stretching a muscle to the point of resistance and holding it in that position) a formal part of the warm-up routine.

"A growing body of evidence," says Dr. Avery Faigenbaum, an exercise scientist at the University of Massachusetts in Boston, "suggests that a more dynamic warm-up period consisting of jumps, lunges, hops, and skips is more fun and more effective than traditional stretching. I recommend dynamic warm-up activities before exercise and static stretching after exercise."

In the absence of a formal program that incorporates those kinds of activities, make sure that all of the movements used during games, matches, or other sports events are simulated during the pre-game or warm-up routines. An example is the quick burst of speed used by a baseball player to run toward first base after hitting the ball. If that movement has not been used during a warm-up period, the scenario exists for a strained hamstring muscle. It is not unusual to see young baseball players (and even major leaguers) stretch during their warm-up periods, then sit or stand for two or more hours before using the muscles they stretched earlier. Common sense would dictate that dynamic stretching activities should continue throughout the game as long as there is a chance a player will participate at some point.

There is a reasonable amount of evidence that stretching increases flexibility and that flexibility indirectly enhances performance because it makes movement more fluid. However, stretching to achieve that goal has to be done on a regular basis (three to four times a week for extended periods of time) rather than just before an event. Many exercise physiologists recommend that traditional stretching, if done at all, should be performed after strenuous activity, not before. Their thinking is that muscles are more pliable and less susceptible to injury when muscle tissue is completely warmed up. Even then, it is possible to injure a weakened or fatigued muscle, so young athletes should stretch under supervised conditions.

The good news about kids and stretching is that they are naturally more flexible than adults. They don't have the muscle mass and the restrictions on movement than adults have developed over a lifetime. For that reason, less emphasis is placed on flexibility training at early ages. Joshua Aycock, a performance specialist at Athletes' Performance in Phoenix, Arizona, doesn't designate a specific amount of time to flexibility training. "We work active and dynamic flexibility exercises into our resistance training routines. For example, if a young athlete does leg curls for the hamstrings, they are followed by a towel stretch to lengthen the same muscles. Pushups are followed by stretches of the pectoral muscles."

The bottom line on stretching for younger athletes and exercisers is to give less attention to formal routines than you would for adults. Instead, incorporate exercises and activities that stretch all the muscle groups into sport-specific warm-ups and resistance training routines.

CHAPTER 2

Selecting the Right Kinds of Stretches

There are hundreds of stretches from which to choose, and there are different ways to execute or conduct each stretch. Understanding the different methods will make it easier for you to choose the type that is right for you.

There are three basic kinds of stretches. Static stretches involve stretching a muscle as far as it will go without pain and holding that position for a few seconds. Ballistic stretches involve continuous bouncing movements. Dynamic stretches are performed at normal speed of movement or at an accelerated pace similar to the movement required to play a sport. Details about each method follow.

Static Stretching

Static stretching occurs when a muscle is stretched to a point of resistance and held for a period of time. It is safe, easy to learn, easy to execute, and has been proven as a means of increasing flexibility. It is also a type of stretching that should play a limited role in your exercise program if you are stretching to improve athletic performance. Why? Because many static stretches not very sport-specific.

Recent studies have shown a slight decrease in muscle strength and power after performing static stretches. Some sports scientists now recommend static stretching 30-60 minutes before an activity begins instead of doing the stretches immediately before an event. Others say that static stretching at any time before a training session or contest is counterproductive to performance. One of the reasons for this view is that static stretches don't involve the rapid movement required in most sports. In other words, static stretches may allow for a greater range of motion in a joint, but not in the high-speed context needed to perform certain sports skills.

But static stretching does play an important role for the average exerciser. It is useful in preventing diminished flexibility in problem areas and in rehabilitation following an injury. It is also recommended after an activity when the body is very warm, making it easier to lengthen muscle tissue. Static stretching after a workout is thought to speed recovery and decrease soreness. The thinking on when to use static stretching may have changed, but the relative importance of its effectiveness has not.

Ballistic Stretching

Imagine a group of exercisers doing ten toe touches without stopping. They bend at the waist, reach down with both hands, and touch their toes—or least try to touch their toes. Then they bob or bounce with each subsequent stretch, trying to increase the range of motion a little more each time. That is ballistic stretching and it is generally not a very good idea. It can cause injury and soreness, and it doesn't allow enough time for the tissues to adapt to the stretch. Instead of relaxing the muscle, it increases tension and makes it hard to stretch the surrounding connective tissues. There are ways to gradually work up to safe ballistic stretches, but for now you have better choices.

Dynamic Stretching

Dynamic stretching involves movement at a normal speed or at the speed required in a sport. You do not hold the stretch at the end of the movement, and you do not bounce or bob.

Traditional warm-up activities such as swinging a baseball bat, a tennis racket, or a golf club are examples of dynamic stretching. Some exercise scientists advise athletes to use dynamic stretches before an activity and static stretches when the major part of the workout has been completed and the person is in a cool-down mode.

Active Stretching

Active stretches include static, ballistic, and dynamic stretching. The term simply means that you complete the stretches without any outside help.

Passive Stretching

In passive stretching, the person doing the stretching relaxes and allows another person (such as an exercise partner or a physical therapist) or a machine to provide the force needed to execute the stretch. You might see passive stretching among teammates before a practice or game or in a rehabilitation session.

Stretches to Avoid

Knowing which stretches to avoid is part common sense and part science. Avoid stretches that you simply cannot do or that put you in a position to hurt yourself. Just because a stretch appears in a book does not mean it is one you should perform. There are stretches that are especially dangerous if they are performed incorrectly or by recreational athletes and exercisers whose bodies are not flexible enough. Among those "red-flag" stretches are deep knee bends, exaggerated lunges, squats, and straight-leg toe touches. Used in the proper setting by well-conditioned athletes, they are an important part of a stretching and flexibility program. Used by others, they may result in an injury.

Which Stretches Are Right for You?

The majority of people who stretch can and should use a combination of static and dynamic stretches—no bobbing, bouncing, or relying on others to do the work. The stretches illustrated in this book can be done alone. They involve either stretching a muscle to a point of resistance and holding it for a specific time period or moving through the range of motion needed to participate in individual or team sports.

Some stretches can actually strengthen muscles at the same time they are being stretched. The weight of a person's body may be enough to provide a training load (as in calf raises). Other stretches may be conducted while supporting weights such as dumbbells or barbells. By the time you look at the exercises and sample programs in this book, you'll know whether you want to stretch for flexibility, for strength, or for both. You don't have to decide now.

In summary, select the stretches that are comfortable, sensible, and practical for your situation. If you are a golfer or tennis player and do your stretching on the practice tee or at the courts, it is not practical to lie down and stretch. There are plenty of stand-up and sit-down stretches that will accomplish the same goal. If you are a young, developing athlete, you probably have the luxury of doing just about any stretch that will help you perform better in your sport. If you are a senior exerciser, choose the ones that you are able to do and that make you feel better. Don't make this complicated, and don't worry about what others do or say. It's your body and your business.

CHAPTER 3

The Rules

There are several guidelines to follow in a stretching program, but they are, pun intended, pretty flexible. Stretching programs should be individual in nature, depending on factors such as your level of fitness, existing flexibility or lack of it, health, lifestyle, age, and especially, your reasons for stretching. Are you trying to develop flexibility, maintain what you already have, or regain the flexibility you had before an injury or illness? Here are the answers to questions about stretching rules.

When?

Regardless of the time of day you choose to stretch, don't stretch first. Although many people think that stretching comes before everything else, it shouldn't. Warm up to loosen up, to raise your body temperature, and to "get the blood flowing" (that is, increase the rate of circulation). Then begin your stretching routine.

There are lots of ways to warm up. Among them are easy calisthenics, walking, jogging, and not-too-stressful bending and twisting movements. Five minutes of warming up will get most people ready to stretch, but you may want to give warming up more time in cold weather, when you are preparing for strenuous training or competition, or if you have a particular part of the body that's a bit slow to start.

Whether by preference or necessity, many exercisers stretch in the morning. It becomes a part of their daily routine and helps them get ready for the rest of the day. Others find that stretching near the end of the day relaxes their muscles. There is certainly nothing wrong with doing both—stretching in the morning and stretching again at night.

Stretching during the workday is an effective way to relieve the physical and mental stress placed on your body and mind. Finding a place at work or school may present logistical problems, but workplace stretches are illustrated in chapter 9. Even if you have to stay at a desk, computer, or other workstation, help is here.

Taking stretch breaks during travel is almost a requirement to avoid stiffness, soreness, or even injury. Sitting for long periods of time in relatively small spaces is not good for any part of the body, but it is especially bad for the lower back. L4 and L5—lumbar vertebrae numbers 4 and 5—support most of the body's weight and are attached to many of the muscles in the back. Those two vertebrae are particularly vulnerable. One way to protect them is to take periodic breaks for stretching the muscles that support the spinal column.

Elite and recreational athletes frequently stretch before training sessions and competition to enhance performance, and afterward to enhance flexibility. Stretching immediately after a workout or game is easier, safer, and more productive than at other times because your body temperature is higher and your muscles are more pliable—easier to elongate. Static stretching for five minutes after exercise prevents muscles from tightening too quickly. Static stretching after a workout is also thought to speed recovery, decrease soreness, and extend muscle length. Some athletes go through an abbreviated version of the same stretches done during the warm-up.

RECOMMENDATION: If you are beginning a stretching program, stretch in the morning. Add other sessions as your body needs them and as your schedule allows them. If you are an athlete, stretch after a warm-up but before a practice or competition, and again after that same training session or game.

How Often?

Stretching at least once a day, every day, is a good habit to develop. However, you can maintain whatever flexibility level you achieve by stretching three, four, or five days a week. Athletes and more serious exercisers sometimes stretch two or three times a day—before, during, and after workouts. And they probably stretch every day, weekends included. While daily stretching sessions are beneficial, you won't revert to your previous level of flexibility if you skip a day now and then or take weekends off. Loss of flexibility takes more time than that.

RECOMMENDATION: Stretch every day, but don't worry if you occasionally miss a session or two.

How Intense?

This is an easy one. Stretch to a point of resistance, but not to a point of pain. That will vary from person to person. It's up to you. Forget the "no pain, no gain" nonsense, whether it's stretching or exercising. If you go too far with a stretch, you won't be able to hold the position long enough to do any good and you run the risk of straining (pulling) a muscle. Follow the advice of Michael Alter, author of Sport Stretch, who says, "Train, don't strain."

RECOMMENDATION: Stretch until you feel tension or resistance, and then hold the stretch before returning to the starting position.

How Long?

The experts are all over the place with the question of how long to hold a stretch. Their suggestions range from six seconds to one minute, but six seconds may not give the muscle time enough to relax in the stretched position. Sixty seconds may not be practical. Completing a series of stretches that each last a minute may take more time than you have or, in the case of athletes warming up for a game, more time than the activity that follows. There is no research that says a stretch held 60 seconds is more beneficial than one that lasts 30 seconds.

RECOMMENDATION: Thirty seconds per stretch seems to be a reasonable compromise. Or, break the 30 seconds down into three ten-second repetitions.

How Many Repetitions Per Stretch?

Sorry, but there is no consensus here, either. Some athletes may do as many as 40 repetitions. Some experts advise ten to fifteen; others, three to six; and still others, two to three repetitions for each muscle or muscle group being extended.

RECOMMENDATION: Two to three repetitions per stretch; more if you are preparing for an event that requires strenuous exercise.

How Many Different Stretches?

There is no set number. It depends on you and why you're doing the stretches. For those who need a general flexibility program, one or two stretches for each major area of the body—1) lower legs/ankles, 2) upper legs, 3) lower back/trunk, 4) upper back/shoulders/neck/arms—makes sense. For athletes or those with special needs, it may be necessary to concentrate on some areas and back off on others.

RECOMMENDATION: Six to eight stretches per session, divided among the upper body, lower body, and trunk.

What About Breathing?

Don't forget to do it. Don't hold your breath. Breathe as normally as possible, always under control. Exhaling may help you relax immediately before each stretch.

Design Your Own Program

Take the information in this chapter and design your own program. Start slowly. Gradually increase any of the variables, but take your time doing it. As with resistance training loads, never increase anything—whether it's frequency, duration, intensity, or any other component—more than ten percent at a time. Soon enough, you'll find a stretching groove that works. Stay with it for six months and you're likely to continue it for the rest of your life.

CHAPTER 4

Stretches for the Lower Body

In this section there are stretches for the muscles, tendons, and ligaments of the feet, ankles, lower legs, knees, upper legs, and hips. Don't try to do all of them. Some are appropriate for beginning exercisers; others are for experienced and more flexible exercisers and athletes. There are descriptions and illustrations that give different ways to stretch the same area. Experiment with various positions and stretches, then select the ones with which you are comfortable. Unless otherwise noted, hold each stretch for 30 seconds or for three, ten-second periods. There will be reminders along the way.

FEET AND ANKLES

1 FEET/TOES In a sitting position, cross one leg over the other. Grasp the ankle with one hand and the toes or ball of the foot with the other. Pull your toes up and back toward your shin to stretch the tissues on the bottom of your foot. Switch legs and repeat.

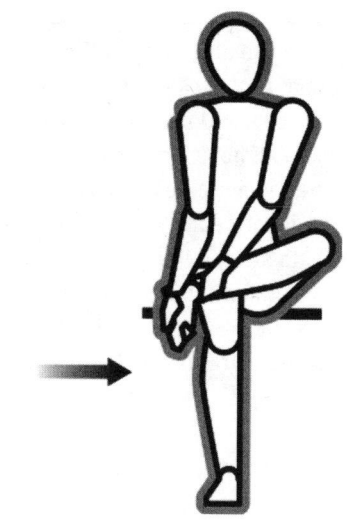

2 **FEET/TOES** Again, in a sitting position, cross one leg over the other. Grasp the ankle with one hand and pull your toes down toward the ball of the foot with the other. Switch legs and repeat.

3 **FEET/ANKLES** In a sitting position, cross one leg over the other. Grasp the ankle with one hand and pull (turn) the sole of your foot toward your body with the other. Switch legs and repeat.

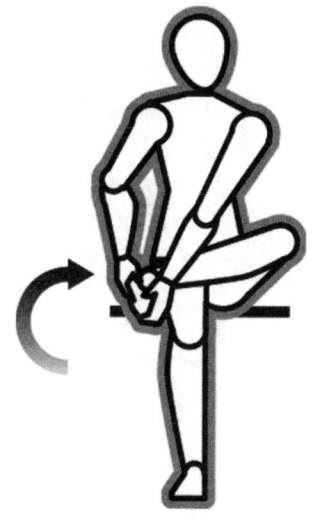

4 FEET/ANKLES Take a sitting position, one leg crossed over the other. Place one hand on the lower leg and the other around the top part of your foot. Rotate your ankle so that the sole of your foot moves away from your body. Switch legs and repeat.

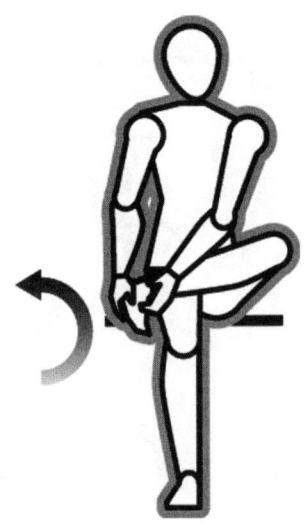

FEET AND ANKLES

5 ANKLES Stand with your feet parallel to each other and wider than your shoulders. Bend the left knee and lean toward the left. Keep your back straight, right leg straight, feet flat on the floor. Hold for three ten-second stretches, then lean to the right.

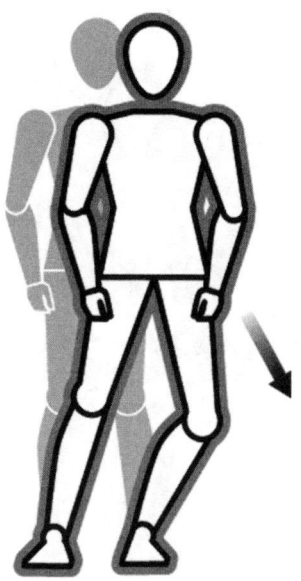

6 ANKLE LEAN This one can be used to stretch the ankle and the sole of the foot. In a standing position, lean forward with both hands touching a wall, one foot forward, the other foot back. Start with the back foot flat on the floor, then raise the heel and shift your weight to the ball of the rear foot. Switch legs and repeat.

7 TOES BACK (DORSIFLEXION) In dorsiflexion, sit in a chair and point the toes back toward the shin to stretch the calf muscles and the band of tissue (fascia) that runs along the bottom of the foot. For an added stretch, reach down, grasp the top of your foot and gently pull it back. Hold for three ten-second periods. This stretch is used to help avoid plantar fasciitis and to alleviate the discomfort after it has developed.

8 TOES DOWN (PLANTAR FLEXION) Sitting position. In plantar flexion, point the toes down toward the floor and hold for three ten-second stretches. This stretch is used by hurdlers and dancers for lower leg and foot flexibility.

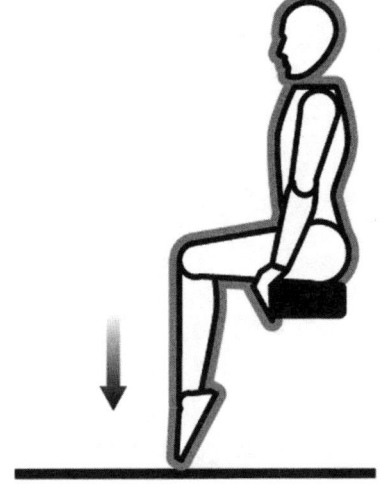

9 FEET/ANKLES Start on your knees, hands touching the floor or mat in front of you, and toes in contact with the floor behind. Slowly shift your weight back and down, sitting on your heels, if possible. Some people are not ready for this stretch. If you are one of those people, gradually work into it or choose another stretch for your feet and ankles.

Lower Legs

The stretches that follow involve the ankles, the area between the ankles and knees, and the knee joint. There are overlaps in these exercises for adjacent parts of the body. Intentionally or not, you might be addressing more than one area at a time.

How Flexible Are You?

To check the flexibility of your Achilles tendons (the bands of tissue that extend from your heels upward) and your calves (the muscles on the back side of the lower leg), sit on the floor with your left leg tucked inward and right leg extended. Reach forward, try to grasp the toes of your right foot, and pull them toward you. The bottom of your foot should form a right angle with the floor. If you can't reach your toes, you have a tight calf and Achilles tendon.

10 **ACHILLES TENDON/CALF** Stand two to three feet from a wall. Lean forward with both hands touching the wall, one foot forward and the other 12-18 inches behind. Leave both feet flat on the floor during the stretch. After a 30-second hold (or three 10-second holds), change the position of your legs and stretch the other Achilles tendon.

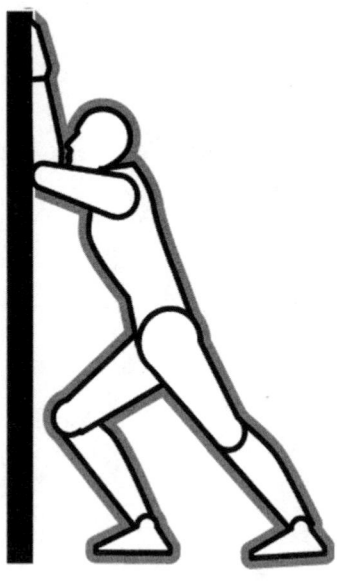

11 ACHILLES WALL Stand three to four feet away from a wall and facing it, feet even (not staggered). Keep both feet flat on the floor and place your hands on a wall at about shoulder height. Shift your weight forward and lean against the wall. Feel the tension on the backsides of your legs.

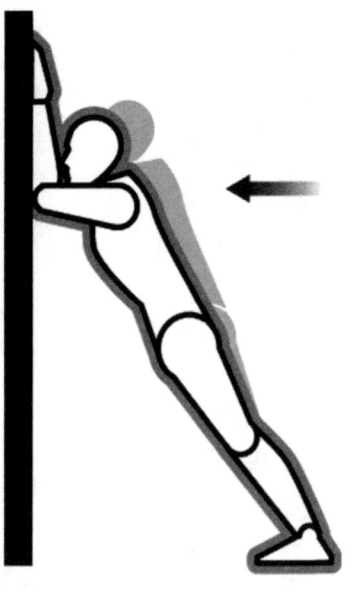

12 ACHILLES TOWEL Lie on your back with your right leg extended on the floor. Loop a towel around the front part of the left foot and extend the leg upward as far as it will go without pain. Pull gently on the towel, pointing your toes back toward your body. Switch legs and repeat.

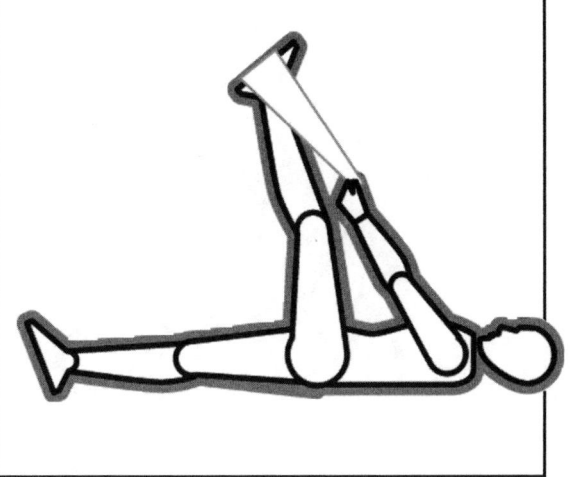

13 **LYING ACHILLES** This is a fourth option for stretching the Achilles tendon as well as the back of the lower leg. Lie on your back. Bend your right leg so that your foot is flat on the floor and as close to your hips as possible. Lift the left leg, grasp it behind the knee with both hands, extend your leg up, and bend your toes toward your body. Hold, then change leg positions and stretch the Achilles tendon in the right leg.

14 CALF RAISE The calf raise and its variations are among the most effective stretches for the muscles of the lower leg. Stand near something (a desk, table, counter top) to hold for support, if necessary. With your feet parallel to each other and spread at shoulder width, rise straight up on your toes to a point of resistance and hold the stretch for ten seconds. Slowly return to the starting position and repeat twice. As with the other stretches, the alternative is to hold for one 30-second period.

Be careful. If you have small feet and a large body, raising too much weight is risky. Over-doing calf raises could also tear the fascia or muscles in the foot. The key is to gradually increase the height of the calf raise.

15 **STAIR-STEP CALF RAISE** Stand on a stair step with the toes of both feet near the edge. Position your heels below the level of the step, then rise on your toes. Hold the stretch and slowly return to the starting position.

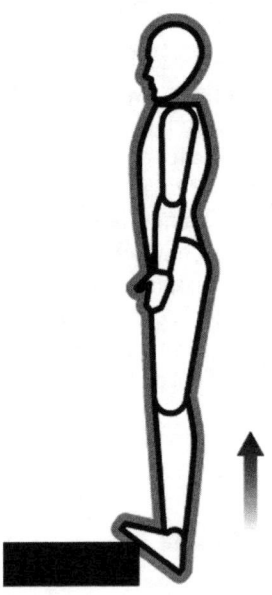

16 **SINGLE-LEG CALF RAISE** Start with your feet flat on the floor and use one hand against a support to steady yourself. Rise as high as possible on one foot. Return to the starting position and rise on the other foot. The illustration shows the exercise as done on a stair step.

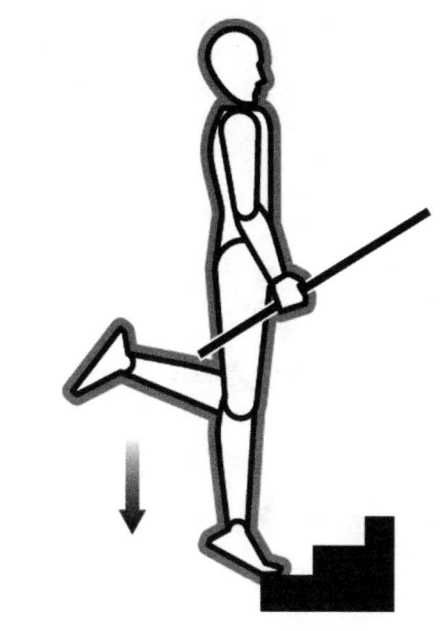

17 **SPREAD LEG** This exercise requires a considerable degree of trunk and hip flexibility, so don't try it unless you are reasonably flexible. Sit on the floor and spread both legs out and to the side at about a 45-degree angle. Bend forward at the waist, reach down, and try to grasp the toes of each foot with the right and left hands, respectively. Then gently pull back. The Spread Leg stretch—if you can reach your toes—is for the ankle joints and the muscles of the lower legs.

18 LUNGE Stand with your feet separated by 12 to 18 inches, one in front of the other (staggered), and toes pointed forward. Slowly shift your weight forward, bending the knee that is out in front and keeping the heel of the back foot on the floor. You should feel resistance in the muscles on the back of the rear leg (calves). Switch legs and repeat.

Upper Legs

The stretches that follow are for the muscles, tendons, and ligaments that begin at the knee (or slightly below it) and extend up the leg to the groin area and hip joint.

Start with the hamstrings. They are the muscles and tendons behind the upper leg and are often strained, or pulled, when a person sprints without warming up and stretching first. When injured, the hamstrings are difficult to treat. The first seven stretches in this section present options. Find one or two that fit your body, or periodically change hamstring stretches to add variety to the program.

19 LYING HAMSTRING Lie on your back, raise one leg, and grasp it with both hands behind your knee (which is bent). Keep the other leg straight. Now straighten the leg you're holding and gently pull it toward your chest. Point your toes toward your head. Switch legs and repeat. This exercise also stretches the gluteal muscles (buttocks).

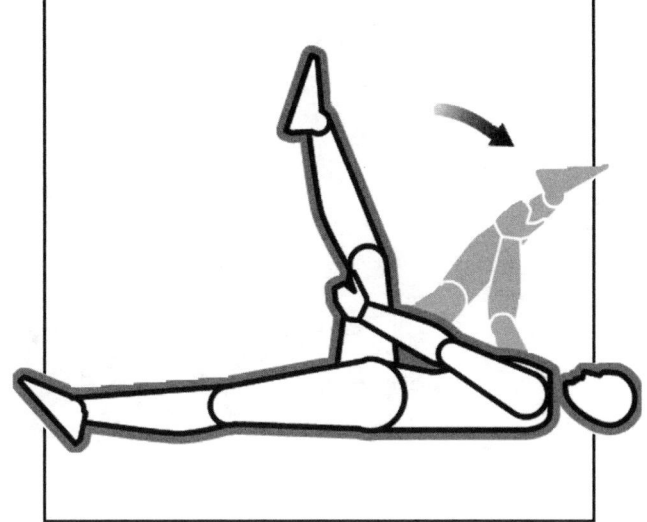

UPPER LEGS

20 PRONE HAMSTRING Lie face down, forehead resting on a folded towel, legs extended, arms at sides. Raise the right leg until you feel resistance, hold the stretch, and lower the leg back to the starting position. Repeat two more times, then do the same lift with the left leg. Or, alternate stretching the right and left legs. A variation is to position your arms on the floor, out in front of your body. As you stretch one leg, lift and stretch the opposite arm for the same count. Repeat with the other leg and arm.

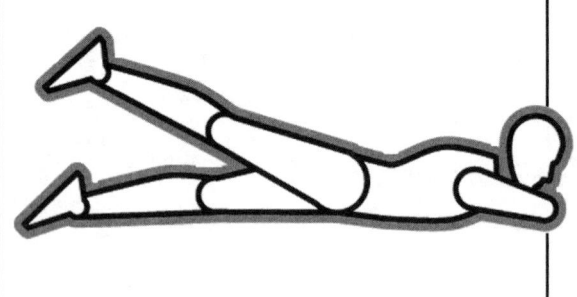

21 PRONE HAMSTRING Lie face down, forehead resting on a folded towel, legs extended, arms at your sides. Flex the left leg and reach back with either hand to grasp the foot or ankle. Gently pull to the point of resistance, hold, release, lower the leg, and repeat twice. Follow the same sequence with the right leg.

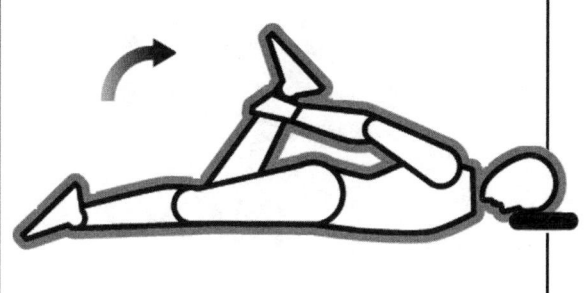

22 SITTING HAMSTRING Sit on the floor with one leg extended straight ahead. Bend the other one so the bottom of your foot touches the inside of the opposite thigh. Lean forward and down toward the straight leg with arms extended toward your foot. Switch legs and repeat. The position for this stretch is similar to the Achilles flexibility test illustrated earlier in this chapter.

UPPER LEGS

23 DOORWAY HAMSTRING In a lying position, in front of and slightly to the side of a door frame, extend the right leg upward and against the door frame as far as possible without discomfort. You may not be able to fully extend the leg, so try to work gradually toward that goal. While the right leg is up, the left leg is extended on the floor and through the doorway opening. Switch legs and repeat.

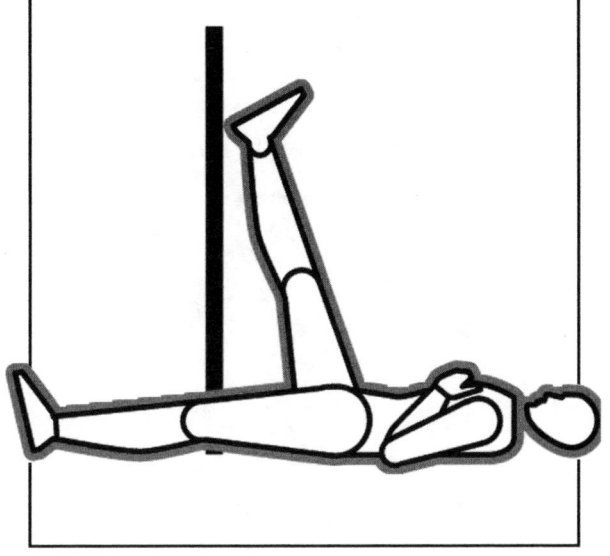

24 HAMSTRING SQUAT STRETCH

Start from a bent-over standing position with your feet flat on the floor, knees flexed, chest close to your thighs, and hands touching the floor (if possible, but don't push it). Exhale and slowly straighten your legs. Don't try to fully extend them if you are not accustomed to the exercise. Hold the position when you feel tension, then gradually return to the starting position.

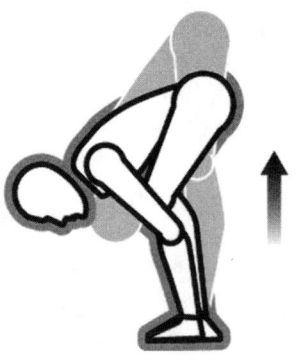

25 **TABLE TOP HAMSTRING** Stand two to three feet from a waist-high table, counter, or bench. Extend your right leg and place your right foot on the table (heel in contact, toes up). Bend at the waist and lower your upper body toward the extended leg. Flex the opposite knee slightly, if necessary, while bending forward. Switch legs and repeat.

26 **ILIOTIBIAL BAND (IB)** The iliotibial band is a tendon that stretches from the outer rim of the pelvis, down the side of the leg, around the outside of the knee, and attaches to the tibia (the shinbone). To stretch the IB, stand with your right hand against a wall and your right leg approximately three feet from the wall. Cross your left leg over the right one. Now gently push your hips toward the wall and hold the position for 30 seconds. Switch supporting legs, and stretch the IB in the other leg. Increase the length of the stretch by standing farther from the wall.

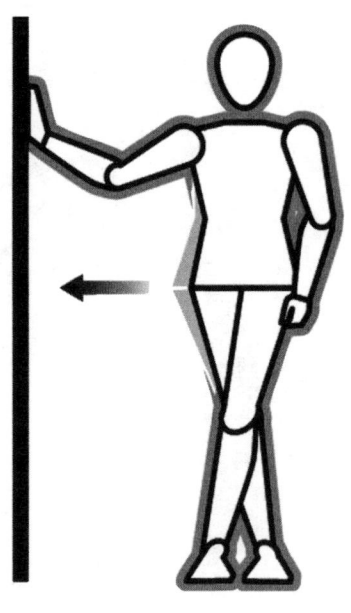

27 ILIOTIBIAL BAND (IB) This stretch is not for a beginning exerciser. Sit on the floor with the right leg extended in front of your body. Then position the foot of the left leg across the top of your right leg and on the floor or mat outside the right knee. Reach across with your right arm and place your elbow against the outside of the left knee. Push it gently to the right and hold for 30 seconds. Switch legs and repeat.

How Flexible Are You?

To test the muscles that flex the hips, lie on your back and draw the left knee to your chest. Continue holding the knee to the chest while extending the right leg until it lies flat on the floor. Repeat the procedure on the other side. If you can't completely extend one leg or if you can't bring the opposite knee to within a few inches of your chest, your hip flexors and buttocks are too tight.

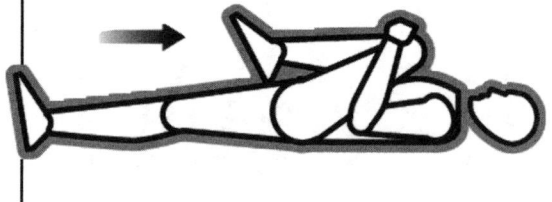

28 SITTING GROIN The groin is an area of the body (the inside of the thigh), not a muscle. The muscles most likely to be injured in the groin area are called the adductors (of the thigh). Some of the activities that require flexible and strong adductors are basketball, cycling, in-line skating, martial arts, rowing, running, racket sports, softball, triathlon, and volleyball.

This stretch requires a degree of flexibility, so don't use it unless you can comfortably assume the starting position. Sit on the floor and position your legs so that the knees are out and the soles of your feet are touching each other. Place your elbows against your knees and press down.

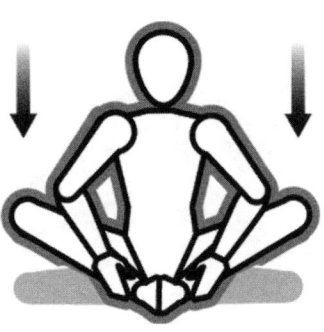

29 ADDUCTOR/GROIN The adductors are muscles in the groin area. This stretch is for conditioned athletes. Sit on the floor or mat, keep your legs straight, and spread them as far as possible. Bend at the waist and reach for your right foot with both hands. Hold for three ten-second counts and return to the starting position before completing two more repetitions. Complete the same bending, leaning, and reaching movement with both hands toward the left foot.

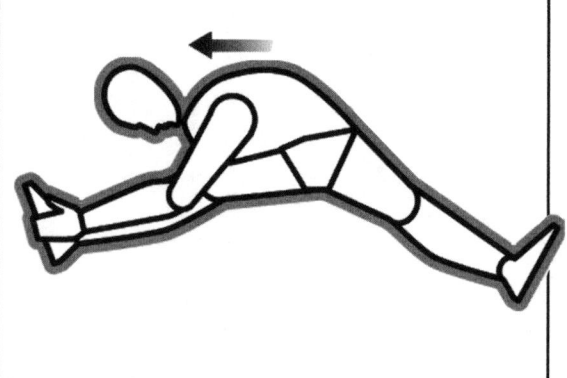

30 GROIN SQUAT Stand close enough to a wall to lean against it. Using the wall to support your back, slowly assume a squat position. Heels slightly apart, toes pointing slightly out, knees above your big toes. Hold onto your toes and position your arms so that your elbows are touching the inside of your knees. Bend forward slightly and carefully push out with your elbows. Do not do this stretch if you have a knee injury or condition that prevents extreme flexion.

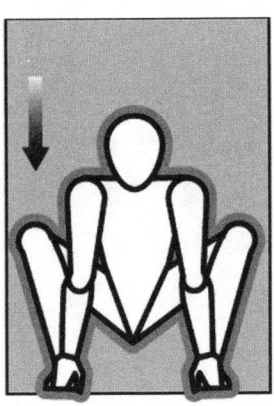

31 STANDING GROIN

Stand with your feet a little wider than your shoulders, hands on hips. Slowly shift your weight to the left, bending the left knee and keeping the right leg straight. At the peak of the stretch, the inside part of your right foot will be in contact with the ground. Repeat to the opposite side. This stretch is similar to Stretch #5, but for a different area of the body.

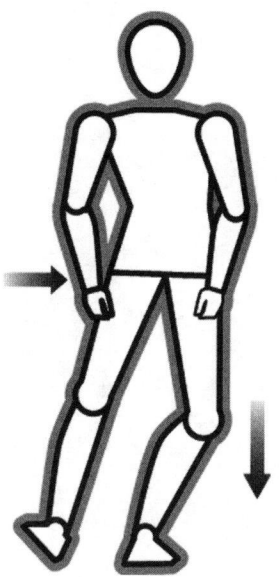

32 LUNGE To stretch the muscles on the insides of the upper legs, stand with your feet separated by 12 to 18 inches, one in front of the other (staggered). Point the toes of the front foot forward, but turn your back foot out with the toes pointing 90 degrees to the side. (The outward position of your back foot makes this stretch serve a different purpose than Lunge #18.) Slowly shift your weight forward, bending the knee that is out in front and keeping the heel of the back foot on the floor. You should feel resistance in the muscles on the back of the rear leg (calves). Switch legs and repeat.

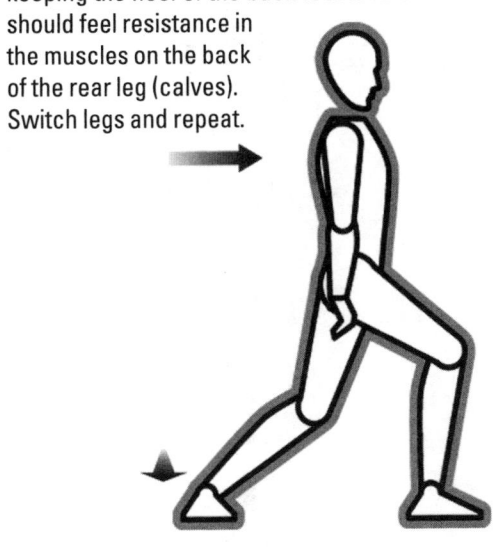

33 **QUADRICEPS STORK STAND** This exercise stretches the quadriceps (muscles on top of the upper leg) and the muscles that flex the hips. Stand on one leg, bend the opposite knee behind your body, and grasp the foot or ankle with either hand. Keep your back straight, bend your knee toward the buttocks, and point the knee to the floor. Don't twist anything. Switch legs and repeat.

34 QUADRICEPS STOOL

Start with your left foot on the floor and the top of your right foot resting on a stool or chair behind you. Keep your upper legs close together as you slowly bend your left knee (as in a lunge movement) until you feel tension in the quadriceps. Keep your back straight. Switch legs and repeat.

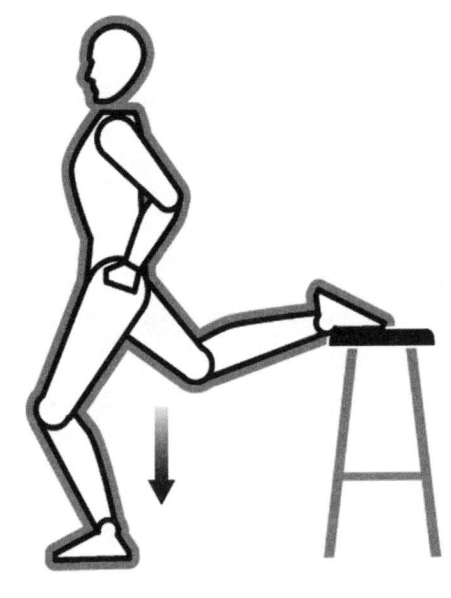

35 **QUADRICEPS LEG RAISE** Lying on your back, bend the knee of one leg and place the bottom of your foot on the floor. Place your arms and hands along each side of your body. Start with the opposite leg extended on the floor. Raise it until you feel tension in the quadriceps. Switch legs and repeat.

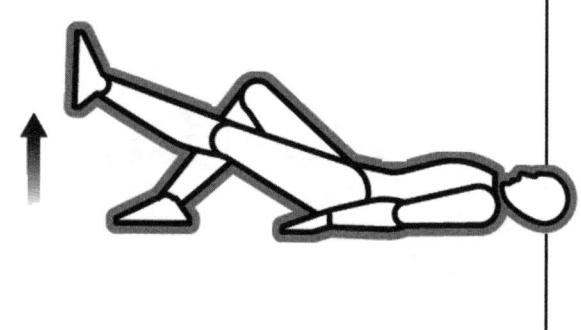

36 TABLE TOP QUADRICEPS Lie on a table or bench, face up, with your left leg near the edge and your right knee flexed, right foot flat on the table. Hold your right leg on the underside (where the hamstrings are located). Relax and let the left leg move off the table top. Bend it at the knee and grasp your foot with your left hand. Pull your leg toward your buttock. Feel the stretch in the middle or upper thigh (quadriceps) To avoid a vulnerable position in the lower back, lift your head and tighten your abdominal muscles. Switch legs and repeat.

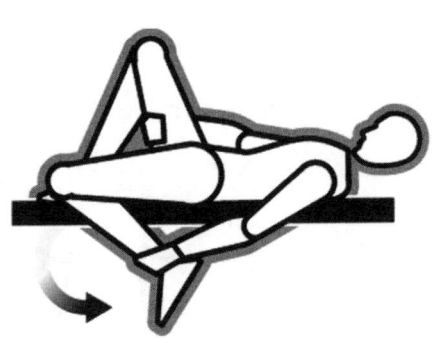

37 LEG LIFT Lie on your left side, right leg resting on the left one. Raise the right leg, hold it for three ten-second stretches, and slowly return to the starting position. Change positions and lift the left leg.

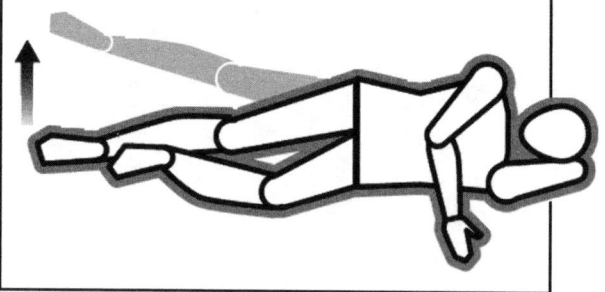

38 **TABLE-TOP HIP FLEX** This stretch is for a muscle in front of the hip that enables it to flex. It's not for those just beginning a stretching program. Stand in front of a table, rail, or bench that is about waist high. Keep your left leg straight, lift your right leg, and place your right foot on the edge of the table. Slowly lean forward. Hold for 30 seconds or for three ten-second stretches, change positions, and stretch the other hip flexor.

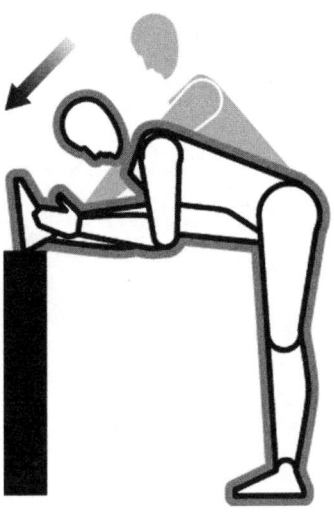

CHAPTER 5

Lower Back and Trunk Stretches

The lower back is a very vulnerable area of the body. Lumbar discs 4 and 5 account for a disproportionate percentage of back injuries. Those who suffer torn or bulging discs, narrowing of the space between the vertebral discs, or strained muscles that support the lower back can perform a variety of stretches to increase flexibility and relieve the pain. Orthopedic surgeons and physical therapists recommend stretches as part of a program to build strength in the lower back.

Core stability has become an increasingly important component of fitness programs. "Core" is a synonym for trunk and "core stability" is the foundation on which total body fitness is built. A core that is strong and flexible can eliminate a lot of potential problems. All the stretches that follow are designed to exercise and increase the flexibility of the lower back and trunk muscles.

How Flexible Are You?

To check the flexibility of your lower back, take your shoes off and stand with your feet together and your knees straight, but not locked. Bend forward and reach for the floor. [DO NOT TRY THIS TEST IF YOU HAVE ANY DOUBT OR QUESTION REGARDING THE CONDITION OF YOUR BACK] Your lower back (and thigh) flexibility is good if you can touch your toes with little effort and no discomfort. If you can touch your toes, but with difficulty, you need work. If you can't even come close to touching your toes, you may be susceptible to lower back injuries and should consult your doctor about a flexibility program.

39 **LYING KNEES-TO-CHEST** This is one of the most widely recommended stretches for people with low back pain or to prevent discomfort in that area. Lie on your back, bend your knees, and hold your legs at a point behind your thighs. Pull your knees toward your chest and slightly raise your hips off the floor. Before you repeat the stretch, slowly move one leg at a time to an extended position.

40 **LYING KNEE-TO-CHEST** Lie on your back with legs extended. Flex the left knee and grasp it with both hands. Pull your bent leg as close to your chest as possible and hold for three ten-second stretches or one 30-second stretch. Return to the starting position and repeat the sequence with the right leg. This stretch is good for the lower back and the muscles that flex the hips.

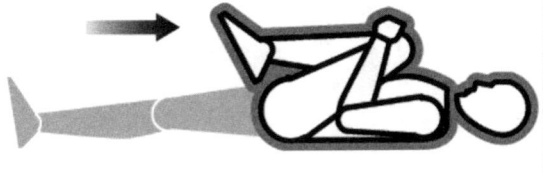

41 **SITTING KNEE-TO-CHEST #41.** Sit in a straight chair, feet on the floor. Grasp your left knee with both hands and bring your leg up toward your chest. Hold, return to the starting position, and repeat (or alternate with the right leg).

42 FULL BODY Lie on your back with your legs extended downward and your arms extended above your head. Try to make your body longer by stretching your legs as far as they can reach while extending your arms in the opposite direction.

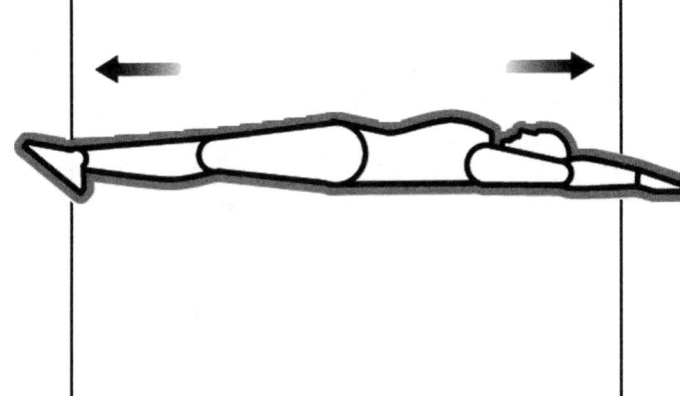

43 **SITTING LOWER BACK** This stretch is good for relieving or possibly even preventing lower back pain. It extends the same muscles as the Knees-to-Chest stretches already described, but provides your body more support and gives you more control. Sit in a chair with your legs bent at the knees and slightly apart. Relax your lower back, bend at the hips, and let your arms hang toward the floor. Bend forward until your stomach touches your thighs.

44 STANDING FLAT BACK Stand up. Keep your legs straight and hold your hands at your sides. Bend forward at the hips, sliding your hands down to a position on your knees. Keep your back flat. Bend your knees or allow your back to relax (not flat) as you return to the starting position.

45 WALL SQUAT Stand close enough to a wall to lean back against it. Using the wall to support your back, slowly assume a modified squat position. Heels apart, toes pointing slightly out, knees above your big toes, and hands resting on your knees. Don't try this stretch if you have a knee injury or condition that could be aggravated by a knee bend position.

46 **CRUNCH** Lie on your back, feet flat on the floor and arms crossed in front of your chest. Raise your head and shoulders slightly off the floor. Hold for ten seconds, return to the starting position, and repeat for a total of three repetitions.

47 **HANG TIME** Find a chin-up bar, door arch, or some other fixed structure that will safely support the weight of your body. The support should be lower than head level. Grasp it with both hands, palms facing away from your body. Keep your arms extended, relax, and hang on so that your trunk and back are slightly arched. Your feet should be well behind the curve formed by your body. A modified version of this stretch can also be performed sitting at a desk. Push your chair back from the desk far enough to bend at the waist, extend your arms fully, grasp the desktop, and arch your back.

LOWER BACK

48 MODIFIED PUSHUP Lie down on your stomach and place your hands in a position to do push-ups. Slowly extend your arms, while raising your upper body, head back. Leave the lower part of your body flat on the floor. At the peak of your stretch, your back should form a slight arch.

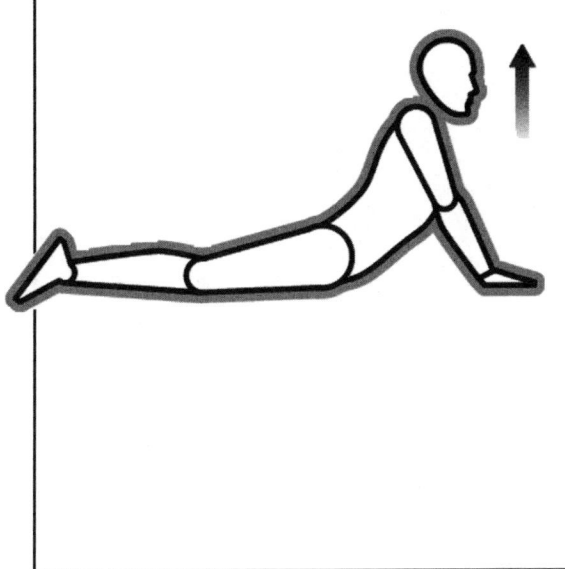

49 **ELBOW PROP** Assume the same position as in the Modified Pushup #48. Instead of extending your arms fully, let the weight of your upper body rest on your elbows. This stretch has been used to ease back spasms.

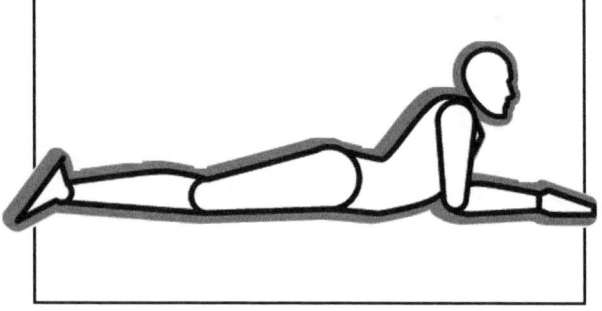

50 **BACKWARD BEND** Stand straight up, feet spread slightly wider than your shoulders, with hands on hips. Relax and gradually bend backward to form an arch with your upper body. Push your hips forward as you bend backward. To increase the difficulty, hold your head back and slowly move your hands down and behind the back sides of your legs.

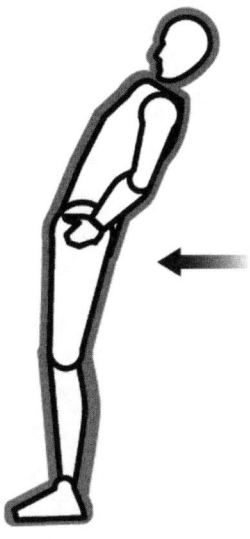

51 **LYING TWIST** Lie on your back, knees bent, feet together and flat on the floor. Keep your feet in the same place and rotate your lower body all the way to the right side so that your right leg touches the floor. Your left leg will be resting on the right one. Hold the stretch, then rotate all the way to the left side. To make it a dynamic stretch, rotate your legs back and forth from right to left instead of holding the stretch in one position.

52 **SITTING TWIST** Sit erect in a straight chair. Cross your arms in front of your chest and rotate your shoulders as far to the left as you can without discomfort. Hold, return to the starting position, and repeat at least two more times. Then rotate to the right. As you get used to the stretch, try to gradually increase the degree of rotation.

53 **STANDING TWIST** Stand erect and cross your arms in front of your chest. Rotate your shoulders as far to the left as possible without pain, hold, and return to the starting position. Repeat twice and rotate to the right. Golfers, tennis players, and baseball players can hold a club, racket, or bat behind their backs or across their shoulders and execute the same movement.

54 **BACK ARCH** Assume an "all fours" position on the floor (on hands and knees). Start with your back in a more or less straight position parallel to the floor before making an upward, rounded arch with your back.

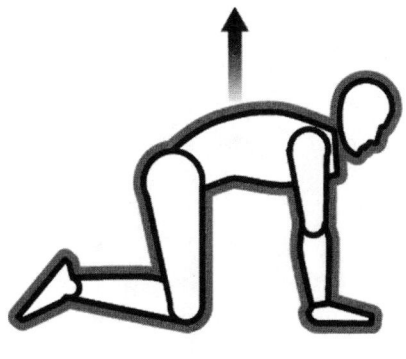

55 STANDING SIDE BEND Stand up, extend your arms upward, and put your hands together above your head. Bend from the hips to your left and down. Hold, return, and bend to the right. This stretch works for golfers, tennis players, and others who need flexibility in the trunk. You can do the stretch holding a tennis racket or golf club above your head to begin the stretch.

56 **BRIDGE** Lie on your back, knees bent, feet flat on the floor. With your back maintaining contact with the floor for support, lift your hips off the floor and hold for ten seconds.

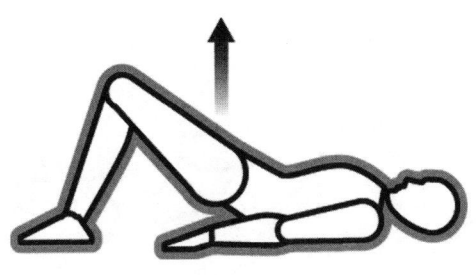

57 **PELVIC TILT** Lie on your back with knees bent and feet flat on the floor. Tighten your lower abdominal muscles and buttocks and press the lower part of your back against the floor. Don't hold this one for 30 seconds. Instead, complete three ten-second stretches.

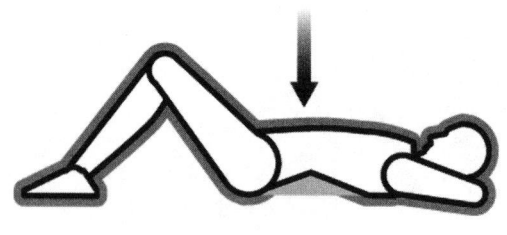

58 **PARTIAL SQUAT** Stand with your feet at shoulder width, toes pointing straight ahead, and feet flat on the floor. To stretch the lower back, hips, groin and hamstrings, slightly bend your knees and hold the position for 30 seconds. Do not bend to the point at which your upper legs would be parallel to the floor.

59 **SITTING SIDE BEND** Sitting in a straight chair, put your hands behind your head. Bend to the right and lower your right elbow toward your right knee. While bending to the right, keep your left shoulder and elbow back. Hold, then bend to the opposite side.

60 **LYING LEG CROSS** Lie on your back. Turn your head to the left as you bend the left leg and bring it over the right leg, across, and down to the right side. To achieve a greater stretch, use your right hand to grasp the left leg and assist in the stretch. Switch legs and repeat.

CHAPTER 6

Stretches for the Upper Body

Everyday fatigue, stiffness, soreness, and stress seem to go straight to the shoulders, neck, and upper part of the back. The stretches that follow should help you avoid or at least relieve some of those problems. There are several for each joint or muscle group, so select the ones right for you.

How Flexible Are You?

To test the flexibility of your shoulder joints, reach your right hand behind your back and your left hand across your back toward your right shoulder blade. Try to clasp your hands together behind your back. If you aren't within an inch of making contact, you might be susceptible to shoulder and neck pain. Increasing your shoulder flexibility will help.

61 ROTATOR CUFF (FRONT) Exercisers and athletes who throw, swing, swim, row, or lift put a lot of stress on the shoulder. The area in the shoulder known as the rotator cuff is made up of four muscles, none of which has a name most people are likely to recognize or remember. There are also other tissues around those muscles that can become irritated and inflamed. The four rotator cuff stretches are often prescribed once an injury has been diagnosed.

Standing up, extend both arms behind your back and clasp your hands together with palms facing out. You should feel pressure as the shoulder blades move toward each other. Get an additional stretch by bending at the waist and raising your arms.

62 ROTATOR CUFF (BACK) There are three ways to do this stretch. Standing or sitting, move one arm into a position that crosses your chest. Grasp your elbow with the opposite hand. Pull the arm straight across your chest, pull it across and down, or alternately pull across then down. Change positions and pull the other elbow.

63 ROTATOR CUFF (UNDERSIDE) Standing or sitting, position the right elbow behind your head, arm bent, and hand in the middle of the back between the shoulder blades. Use the other hand to pull the elbow to the left. It won't take much of a pull to feel resistance, so take it easy. Change positions and pull the left elbow to the right. Gradually increase the distance that the elbow is moved in either direction.

64 **ROTATOR CUFF** Hold the end of a towel in your right hand behind your head. Grasp the end of the towel hanging behind your back with the opposite hand. Now pull upward on the towel with the right hand. Stretch for ten seconds and repeat twice before changing positions.

65 **CHEST STRETCH** To stretch the pectoral (chest) muscles, stand in front of an open doorway with feet staggered and raise your upper arms so that they are parallel to the floor. Place your palms against the frame of the door. Lean forward and hold the position.

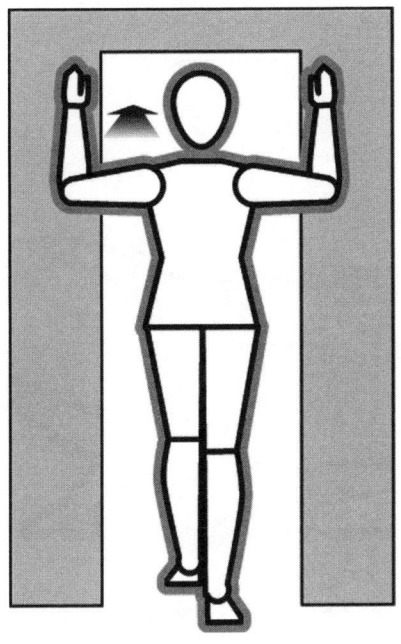

66 UPPER BACK Stand with your feet together approximately three feet from a bar or other support structure that is about shoulder height. Keep your arms and legs straight. Reach forward to grasp the bar with both hands and let your back arch into a swayback position. You can perform a variation on this stretch by pushing your chair away from your desk, holding the edge of your desk, and relaxing into an arched position.

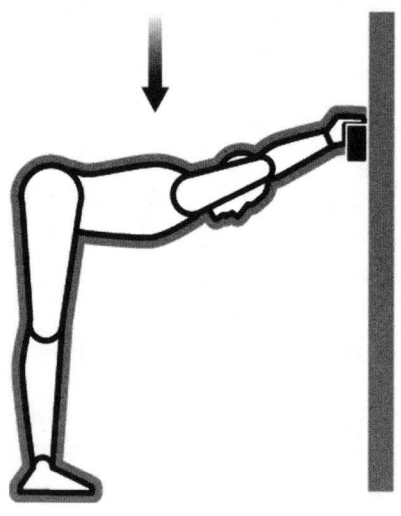

67 **DOORWAY TURN** Stand near the side of a doorway with your feet staggered. Flex the elbow of your left arm and place your palm on the doorframe (or wall) just above head level. Now, slowly turn your upper body away and to the right while keeping your left arm in a fixed position. Switch sides and repeat.

68 ELBOW PULL Put your left arm behind your back in a flexed position. Grasp it with your right hand and pull your elbow across the midline of your back (or at least in that direction). If you can't reach your elbow with the opposite hand, hold your wrist instead. Switch sides and repeat.

69 **SHOULDER SQUEEZE** Sitting or standing, place both hands behind your head. Push your elbows back and squeeze your shoulder blades together.

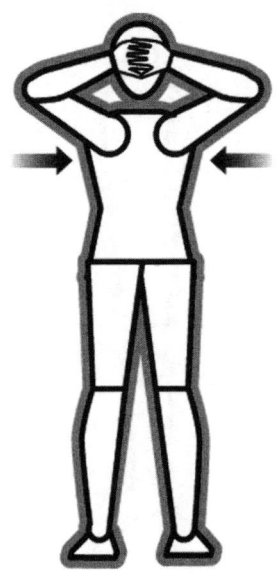

70 **OVERHEAD SHOULDER** Stand up or sit down. Reach up with both arms and clasp your hands above your head. Stretch upward and back to a point where your elbows are behind your ears. Hold for 30 seconds or for three ten-second periods.

71 DOORWAY SHOULDER Use both hands to hold the sides of a doorway frame. With feet parallel to each other, your hands should be behind you at shoulder level and comfortably extended. Lean forward, chest out, chin in.

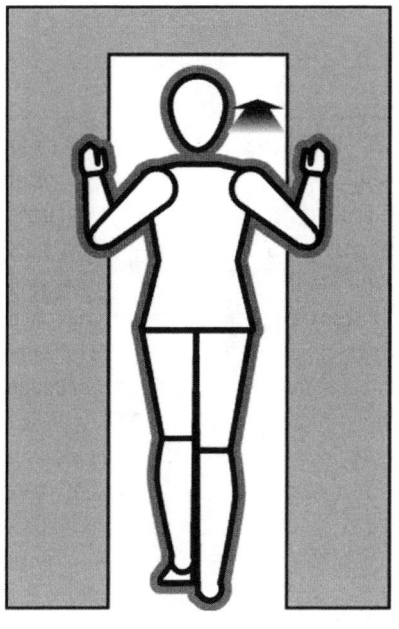

72 FORWARD SHOULDER Interlock your fingers, arms forward at about chest height, palms facing away from your body. Extend your arms as far forward as possible to get a stretch for everything from your shoulders and upper back to your fingers.

73 SHOULDER SHRUG From a standing position, start with your arms down at your sides. Lift your shoulders upward and hold for three ten-second counts or one 30-second count. This stretch is more challenging when you hold a light-weight dumbbell (3-8 pounds) in each hand.

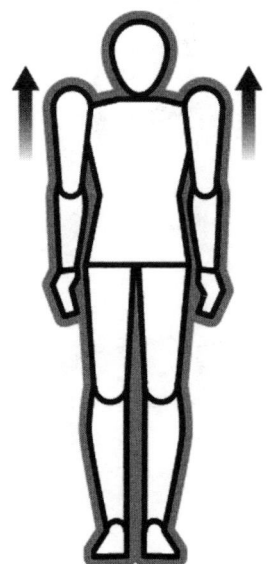

74 **UPWARD SHOULDER** Interlock your fingers. Lift your arms and rotate your wrists so the palms are facing the sky. Extend your arms as far upward as possible. You should feel a stretch in the upper part of your back and the shoulders.

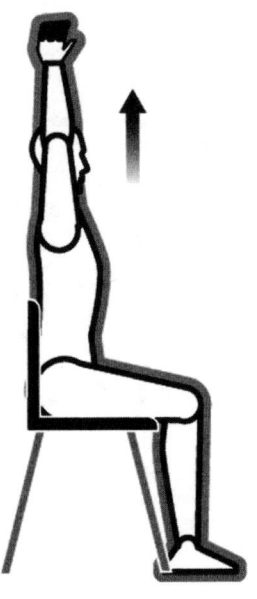

75 **SIT BACK, LEAN BACK** Sit in a chair with a straight back that extends to the middle of your back. Lock your fingers and put your hands behind your head. Lean back and move your arms back at the same time. Get a better stretch by placing a rolled-up towel between mid-back and the chair.

76 SIT FORWARD, LEAN FORWARD Sit on a stool, bench, or chair with your legs together and feet flat on the floor. Put your hands on your hips with your thumbs pointing forward. Bend forward and move your shoulders as close to your knees as possible. As you do, also move your elbows forward and hold the position.

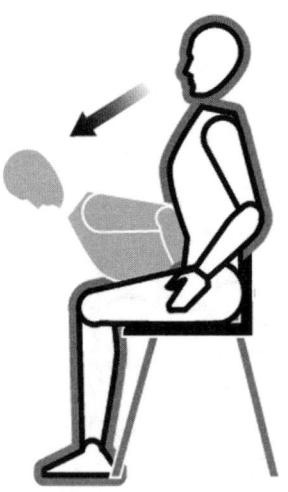

77 LYING NECK Lie on your back with feet on the floor and knees flexed. Interlock the fingers of both hands behind your head, then pull your head toward your chest. Keep your upper back in contact with the floor or mat.

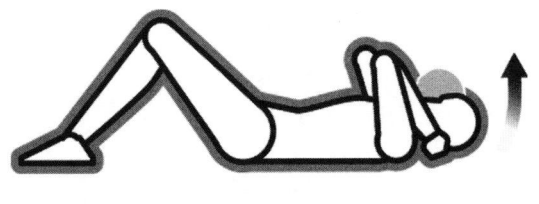

78 FORWARD NECK Sitting or standing, place your hands behind your head. Pull your head downward so that the chin moves down to touch the chest. To stretch against resistance, put your hand on your forehead. Try to touch your chest with your chin, but resist with the hand.

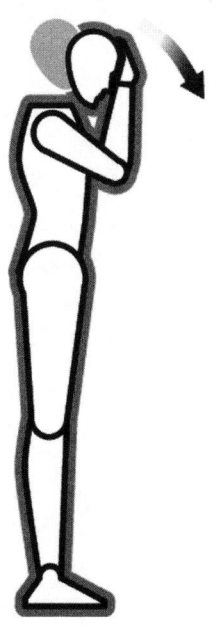

79 SIDE-TO-SIDE NECK Sitting or standing, place your left hand on the left side of your head. Move or pull your head down and toward your left shoulder, hold, and either repeat twice or change positions to pull your head toward the opposite shoulder. Hold the seat of the chair with the opposite hand. To push instead of pull, place your hand on the side of your head and push down with your head against the pressure of your hand.

80 BACKWARD NECK Sitting or standing, slowly and carefully rotate your head and neck back. This stretch is appropriate for wrestlers and martial arts athletes, but others should use caution.

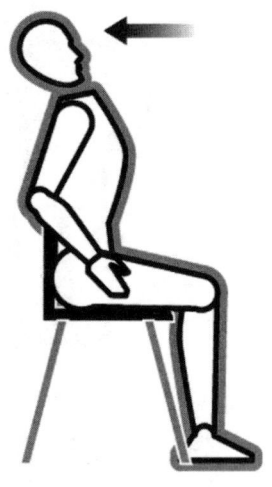

81 **BACKWARD NECK** Lie (on your back) across a firm bed or table and let your head hang over the side. Relax your shoulders and neck while holding the position for 30 seconds.

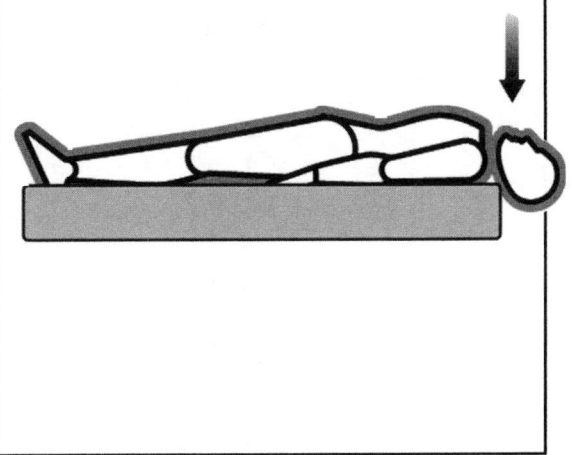

82 **FOREARM** To stretch the muscles on top of the forearm, stand or sit, and extend an arm forward, palm down. Use one hand to firmly push the other hand down toward the floor. Resist with the bottom hand. Keep your arm straight. Switch arms and repeat.

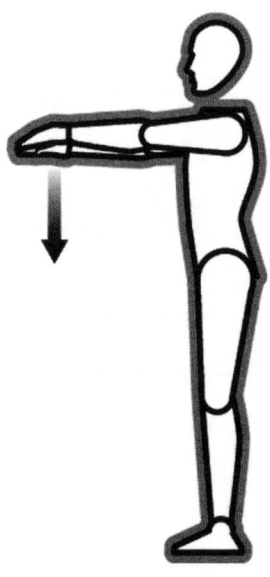

83 **FOREARM** To stretch the muscles on the underside of the arm, extend the either arm forward, palm up. Use the other hand to push the hand down toward the floor. Keep your arm straight. Switch arms and repeat.

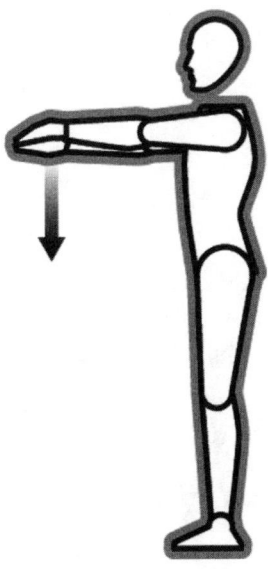

84 **WRIST/HAND** On your hands and knees, place your palms flat on the floor and extend your fingers forward. Slowly lean forward until you feel resistance.

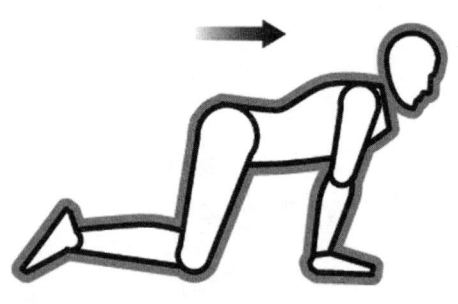

85 WRIST/HAND Standing or sitting, place your palms together in front of your chest, fingers pointing up (as in a praying positon). Now move the heel of one hand up and against the fingers of the other. Push the heel against the fingers. Switch hands and repeat.

CHAPTER 7

Resistance Stretches

You can increase the intensity of stretches with light weights, with elastic bands or cords, or by using an exercise partner to provide resistance. For those who are beginning an exercise program, it is possible to strengthen muscles while they are being stretched. Resistance helps build strength. Well-conditioned exercisers and athletes need a greater load and more repetitions, however, and they have to gradually increase the amount of weight.

Following are examples of stretches with weights for the lower and upper body. The movements are similar to those in previously illustrated stretches. The difference is the added weight. If you are beginning a stretching program, limit the amount of weight to between three and eight pounds.

86 DUMBBELL CALF RAISE

Hold a dumbbell in each hand. With your feet parallel to each other and comfortably spread, rise straight up on your toes and hold the stretch for ten seconds. Slowly return to the starting position and repeat twice.

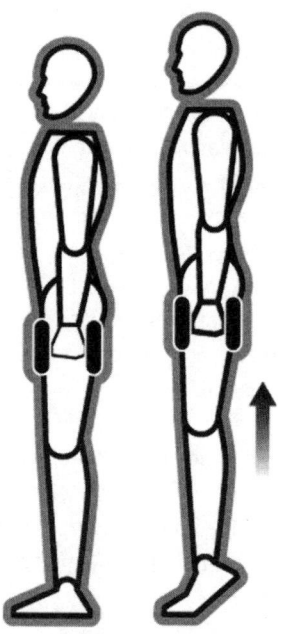

87 ONE-LEG DUMBBELL CALF RAISE Hold

a dumbbell in your left hand and steady your-self by placing your right hand against a wall, chair, or rail. Lift your right foot off the floor and slightly behind your body. Rise on your left foot, hold for ten seconds, and return to the starting position. Repeat twice and change positions to rise on the right foot.

Variation: Hold a dumbbell in each hand while rising alternately on the right and left feet.

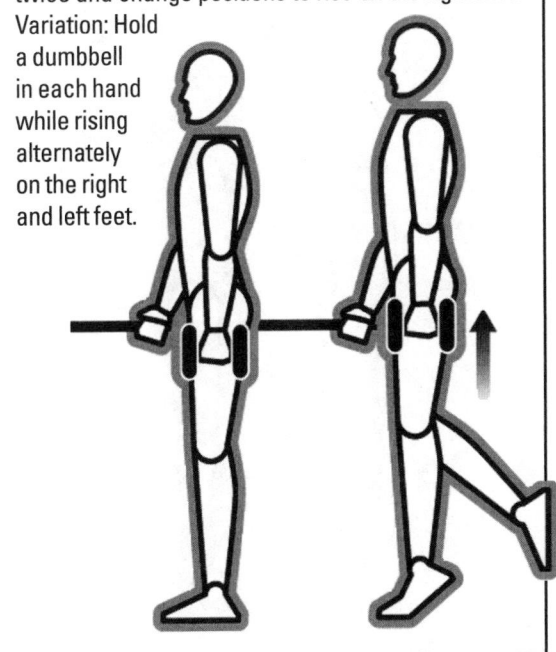

88 STANDING BARBELL CALF RAISE

Have someone help you place a lightweight barbell behind your head, resting on your shoulders. With your feet parallel to each other and slightly spread, rise straight up on your toes to a point of resistance and hold the stretch for ten seconds. Slowly return to the starting position and repeat twice.

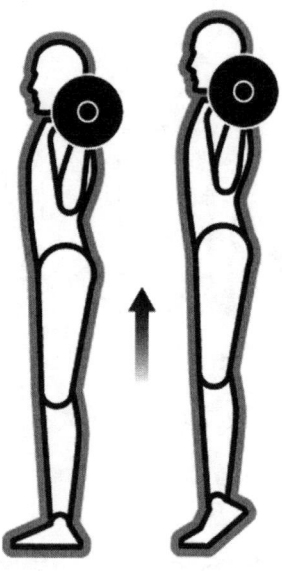

89 TUBED LEG SWING Stand with your right leg two to three feet away from a table or chair that will not move easily. Position your left foot slightly forward. Loop one end of an elastic cord or band around the table or chair leg near the floor and the other end just above your left ankle. Move your leg away from your body, stretching against the resistance of the cord. Hold on to something for support. Switch legs and repeat. This exercise stretches and perhaps strengthens muscles called the abductors. It is also an exercise used for improving balance.

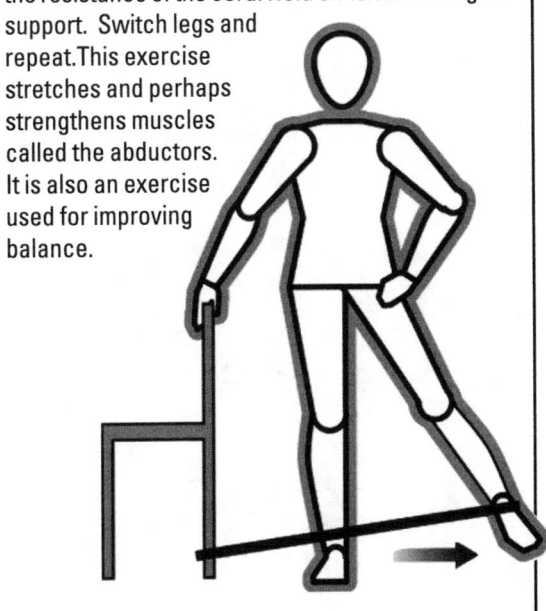

90 TUBED LEG SWING Stand with your left side a few feet away from a fixed support. Loop one end of an elastic cord or band around the support and the other around your left ankle. Stretch the adductor muscles of your legs by pulling against the resistance of the band as you cross your left leg in front of the right one. Switch legs and repeat.

91 **TUBED LEG SWING** Stand with your back a few feet away from a fixed supporting object. Loop one end of a cord, band, or tube around the support and the other around your right ankle. Keep your leg straight and move it forward against the resistance of the tube. Switch legs and repeat. This stretch is effective for the muscles that flex the hip joint.

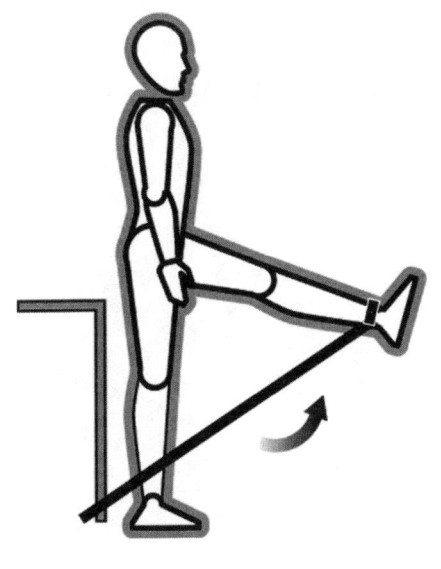

92 **TUBED LEG SWING** Stand facing a fixed object. Loop one end of a tube or band around the object and the other around your ankle. Keep your leg straight and move your leg back against the resistance of the tube. Switch legs and repeat.

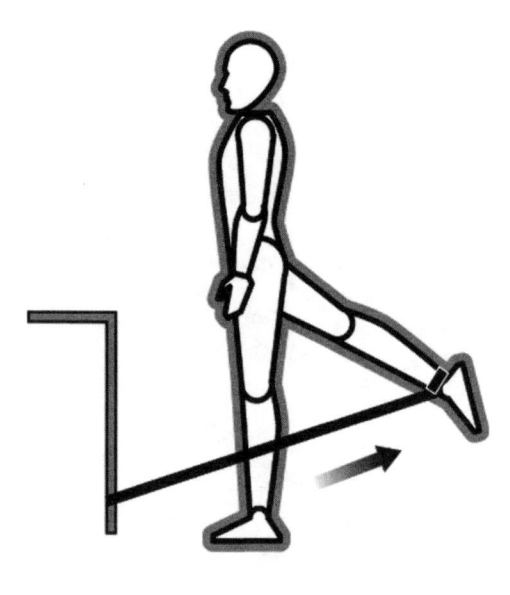

93 **WEIGHTED LEG LIFT** Lie on your side, one leg on top of the other. Secure a 1-3 pound weight around the ankle of the top leg. Lift that leg up and hold the stretch/lift before lowering your leg. After three repetitions, change positions and lift the other weighted leg.

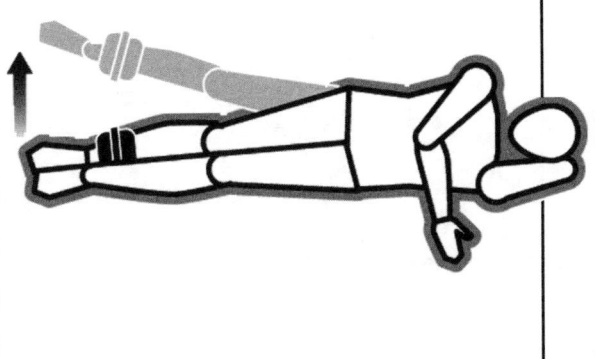

94 WEIGHTED HAMSTRING Lie face down, legs extended, with a light weight wrapped around one or both legs. Bend your knee so that your lower leg moves up, then back toward your body. Repeat the stretch/lift with the other leg.

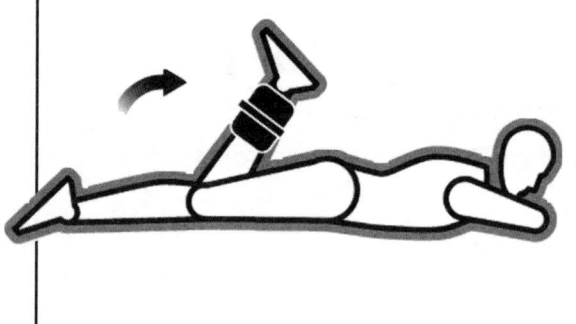

95 WEIGHTED QUADRICEPS LEG RAISE

Lying on your back, bend the knee of one leg so one foot is flat on the floor. Extend your arms along the floor by your sides. Secure a 3-8 pound weight to both ankles. Start with the opposite leg extended on the floor and raise it until you feel tension. Switch legs and repeat.

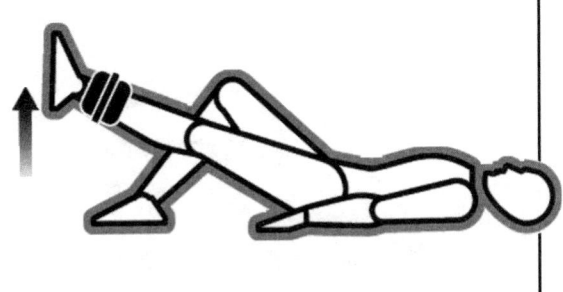

96 **DUMBBELL LUNGE** Stand erect, feet even, with a dumbbell in each hand. Take a long step forward with your right foot to a straddle position in which your right knee is flexed. Hold and return to the starting position, then step forward with the left foot.

97 DUMBBELL SHRUG With arms at your sides, hold a dumbbell in each hand, palms in. Stand with your feet at shoulder width. Elevate your shoulders as high as possible (shrug your shoulders), hold for ten seconds, then lower your shoulders and arms back to the starting position. Repeat the stretch/lift twice. The same stretch can be performed with a barbell instead of dumbbells.

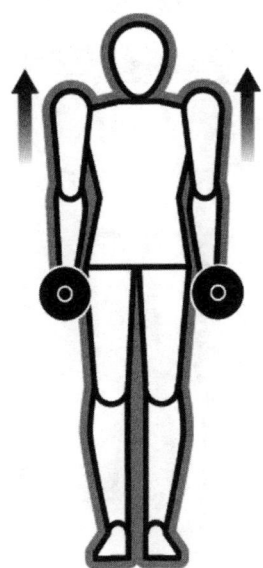

98 **BARBELL BODY TWIST** In a standing position, feet spread at least as wide as your shoulders, rotate the upper part of your body while supporting a barbell on your shoulders. Don't rotate your hips. Carefully and slowly turn first to the right, back to the starting position, then to the left.

99 SEATED ROW For the shoulders, chest, and upper back, sit on the floor or on a stool and loop a resistance band around a secure object. There should be no slack in the band. Keep your hands in the same plane and draw your elbows back as far as possible. Your forearms should remain in a position parallel to the floor during the stretch.

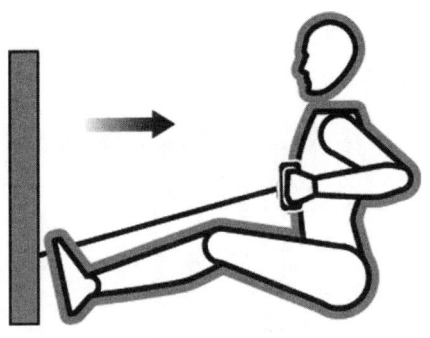

100 **DUMBBELL SIDE BEND** This stretch begins in a standing position with feet parallel and positioned at shoulder width. Put one arm behind your head and hold a lightweight dumbbell (or a similar weight) at your side with the other hand. Slowly bend sideways as far as possible without pain in the direction of the weight you are holding. Switch sides and repeat.

CHAPTER 8

Sport-Specific Stretches

The more a stretch simulates the movement of a sport, the better. The stretches that are included in this chapter are designed for athletes in baseball, basketball, football, golf, running or jogging, skiing, soccer, swimming, tennis, and volleyball. While they don't exactly mimic the movements of the ten sports, they come close and they stretch the most important muscle groups that will be needed for the respective activities.

There are four stretches for each sport, but you can do many more if time permits. They are all described in Chapters 4-7. Consider the four-pack as stretches to get started. Add others to address specific flexibility problems or other areas of the body.

BASEBALL/SOFTBALL STRETCHES

Because the pace of baseball and softball games is slower than in many other sports, the timing of stretches is important. It does little good to stretch an hour or two before batting practice or a game, then sit or stand for long periods before anything happens. With the exception of the pitcher and catcher, both of whom stay a lot busier than the other seven players, it is a good idea to stretch during down times throughout a game. Following are stretches for the hamstrings, groin, upper back, and shoulders. They are Sitting Hamstring #22, Adductor/ Groin #29, Upper Back #66, and Overhead Shoulder #70. If time permits, do as many of the rotator cuff stretches as possible (Stretches #61-#64).

BASEBALL/SOFTBALL STRETCHES

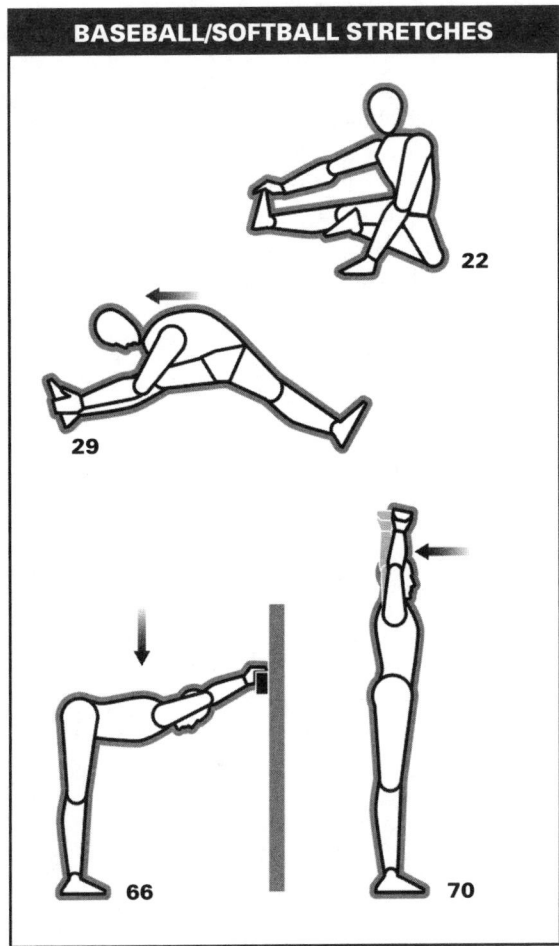

BASKETBALL STRETCHES

With all the physical demands of basketball, four stretches might not be enough to enhance flexibility in every area. Start with the four stretches below and add to them with your choice of stretches for other muscle groups. They are Ankle Lean #6, Calf Raise #14, Chest Stretch #65, and Overhead Shoulder #70.

BASKETBALL STRETCHES

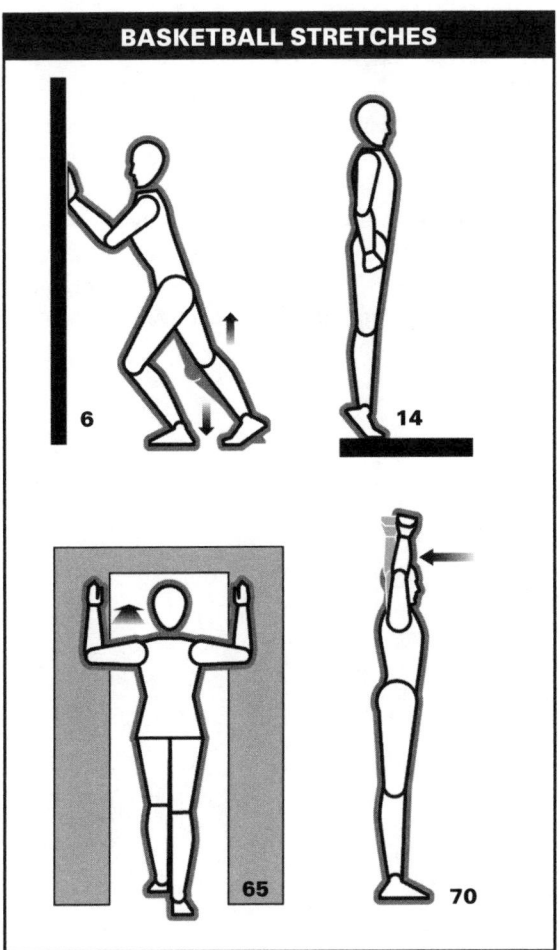

FOOTBALL STRETCHES

Football players need flexibility in the knees, hip, trunk, and upper body to go with the strength that is demanded for blocking, tackling, and running. Stretches for linemen may differ from those for runners, receivers, and defensive backs. Try these four and personalize your routine by adding stretches where you need them most. They are Prone Hamstring #20, Quadriceps Leg Raise #35, Standing Twist #53, and Shoulder Shrug #73.

20

35

53

73

GOLF STRETCHES

At the risk of unfairly criticizing all golfers, they are not exactly famous for taking time to complete a stretching program before they tee off on the first hole. On the practice tee, the practice putting green, or while waiting to drive on the first hole, it is not practical to lie down on the ground for stretches, and there aren't any chairs available for sitting stretches. The result is that many players don't really get loose until the third or fourth hole.

To resolve that problem, Dr. Timothy Hosea, an orthopedic surgeon at the Robert Wood Johnson Medical School in New Jersey, designed a ten-minute warm-up that includes the following four stretches. They are, Standing Flat Back #44, Standing Twist #53, Standing Side Bend #55, and Back Rotator Cuff #62.

GOLF STRETCHES

44

53

55

62

RUNNING/JOGGING STRETCHES

Joggers have a way of warming up as they go. They don't normally charge out of the house or gym at full speed in a way that would risk an injury. Or at least, they shouldn't. For many, a gradual increase in the pace at which they run takes the place of warming up and stretching. However, for those who take the time to stretch before they run, here are four exercises that extend the muscles of the legs: They are Ankles #5, Achilles Wall #11, Calf Raise #14, and Quadriceps Stork Stand #33. If you have time for one more, add Table Top Hamstring #25.

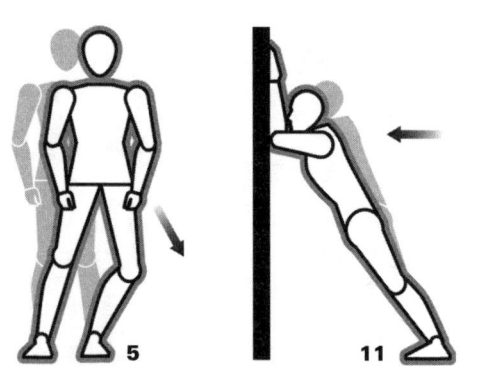

RUNNING/JOGGING STRETCHES

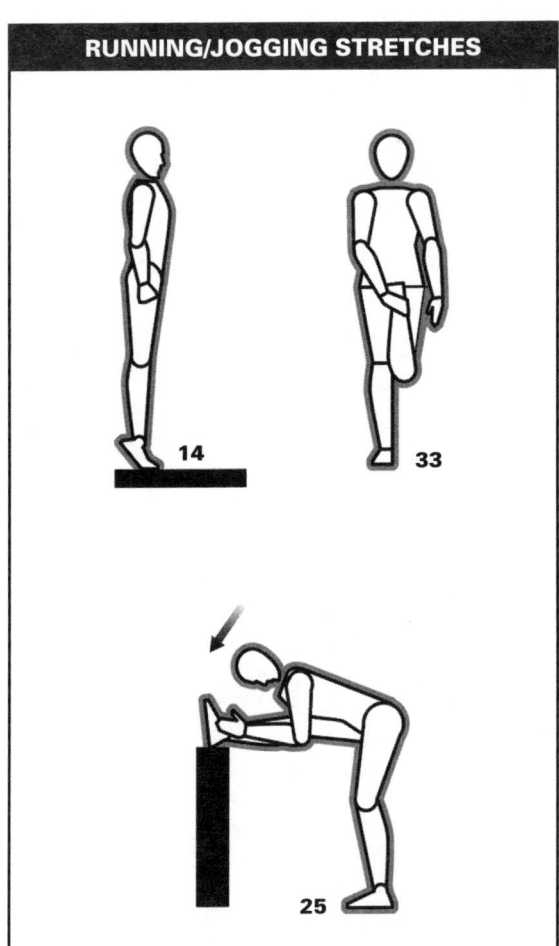

It wouldn't hurt skiers to stretch every muscle in the body, but there is not enough time for that. The stretches here are for the hamstrings, the adductors, the quadriceps, and the lower part of the trunk. Lunge #18 (or #32), Standing Groin #31, Quadriceps Stork Stand #33, and Standing Twist #53.

SKIING STRETCHES

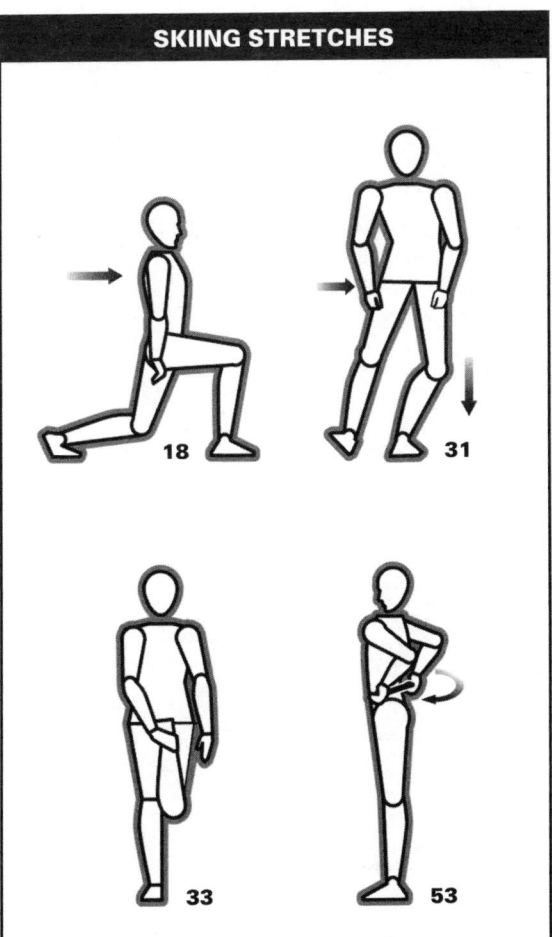

SOCCER STRETCHES

Although the muscles and joints of the upper body get plenty of action during a soccer game, most of the work is done from the waist down. The four stretches at right all involve the lower body: the ankles, knees, hamstrings, and groin muscles, among others. They are Prone Hamstring #20, Sitting Groin #28, Adductor/Groin #29, and Quadriceps Leg Raise #35.

SOCCER STRETCHES

20

28

29

35

SWIMMING STRETCHES

The exercises illustrated below stretch the hamstrings, groin, shoulders, and upper back. They are Prone Hamstring #20, Adductor/Groin #29, Leg Lift #37, and Upper Back #66. Swimmer's shoulder is a loosely-defined injury that includes a lot of things that could go wrong. Adding any or all of the rotator cuff stretches #61 and #64 would be a good idea.

SWIMMING STRETCHES

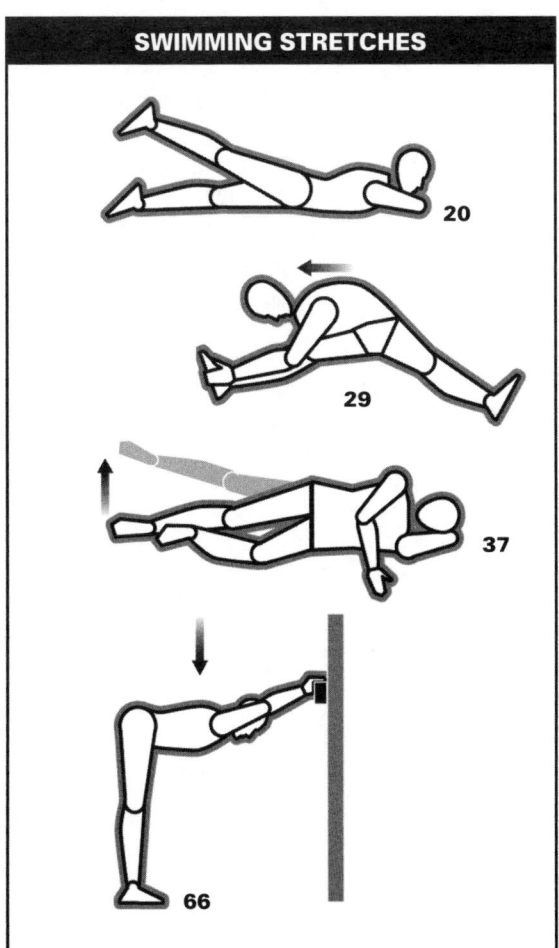

TENNIS STRETCHES

The United States Tennis Association recommends 21 stretches in its book, *Complete Conditioning for Tennis*. Following are four of those stretches that serve as a foundation for upper and lower body flexibility. They are Achilles Tendon/Calf #10, Standing Groin #31, Standing Side Bend #55, and Shoulder Squeeze #69.

TENNIS STRETCHES

VOLLEYBALL STRETCHES

Volleyball players can choose from more than 50 stretches, all of which would help get them ready for practice or games. Michael Alter, author of Sport Stretch, recommends the four below for the feet, ankles, adductor muscles, lower back, arms, and wrists. They are Ankle Lean #6, Adductor Groin #29, Sitting Lower Back #43, and Elbow Pull #68.

VOLLEYBALL STRETCHES

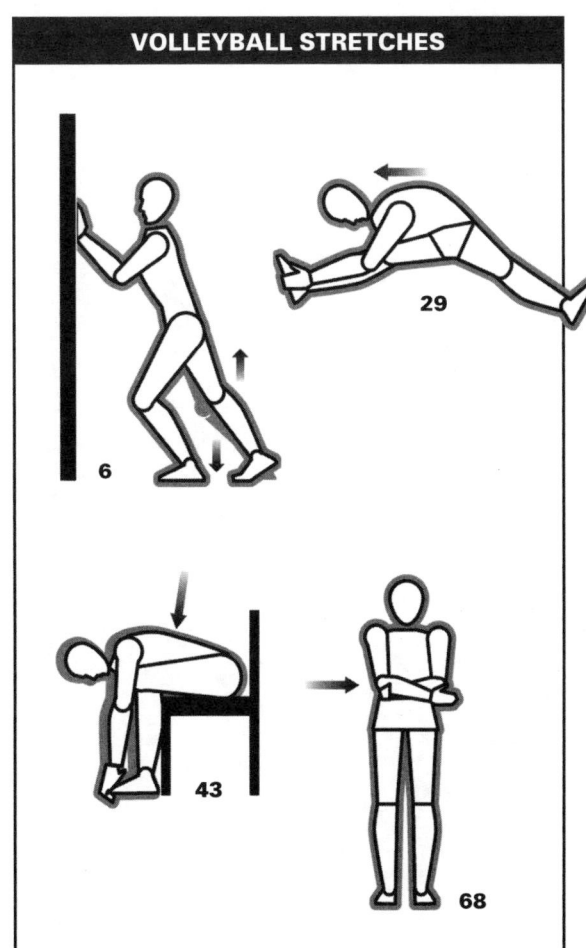

CHAPTER 9

Special Situation Stretches

There are certain conditions and situations in which stretching is particularly helpful in preventing or relieving sore and stiff muscles. Not stretching might even make an existing condition worse.

This section begins with a sample program for novices and continues with stretches that can be performed at a desk, while watching television, or while traveling in a car or plane. There are also programs for those with bad backs, aching shoulders, and stiff knees or legs. Four stretches for each special situation are illustrated here. For detailed explanations of the stretches and to choose from more options, use the stretch number given here and refer back to the same number in chapters 4, 5, 6, and 7.

BEGINNING-A-PROGRAM STRETCHES

If you have never engaged in a systematic program of stretches, start slowly and choose your stretches carefully. Many of the stretches in this book offer sitting, standing, and lying options. Choose the ones that you can do comfortably for the lower body, trunk, and upper body. There is no need to rush into more challenging exercises. If there is any question whether a stretch could have an adverse affect on your health, check with your doctor first. Following are four to get you started: Achilles Wall #11 (for the lower legs), Lunge #18 or #32 (for the upper legs), Sitting Knee-to-Chest #41 (for the lower back), and Doorway Shoulder #71 (for the shoulders and upper back).

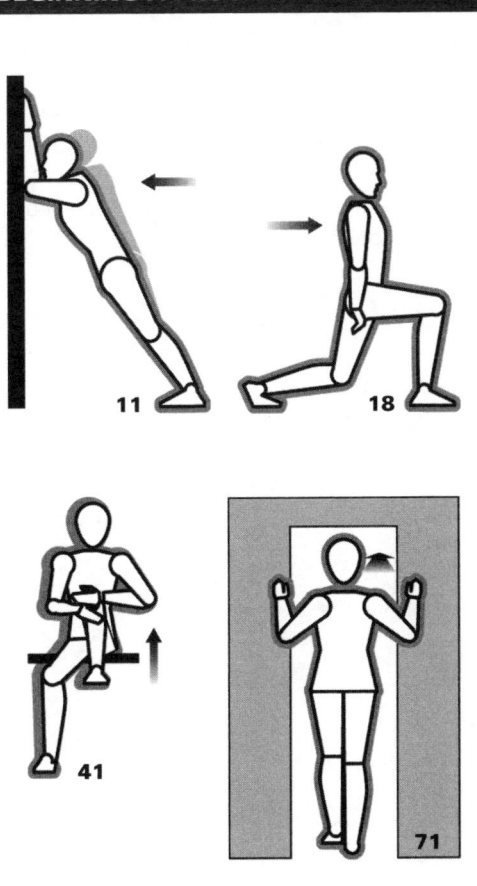

SITTING-AT-A-DESK STRETCHES

A sure way to end up with sore shoulders and back pain is to sit at a desk all day, especially if you are working at a computer. Here is one stretch for the lower body and three for the upper body and shoulders: Sitting Knee-to-Chest #41, Upper Back #66, Shoulder Squeeze #69, and Overhead Shoulder #70 (or Shoulder Shrug #73).

SITTING-AT-A-DESK STRETCHES

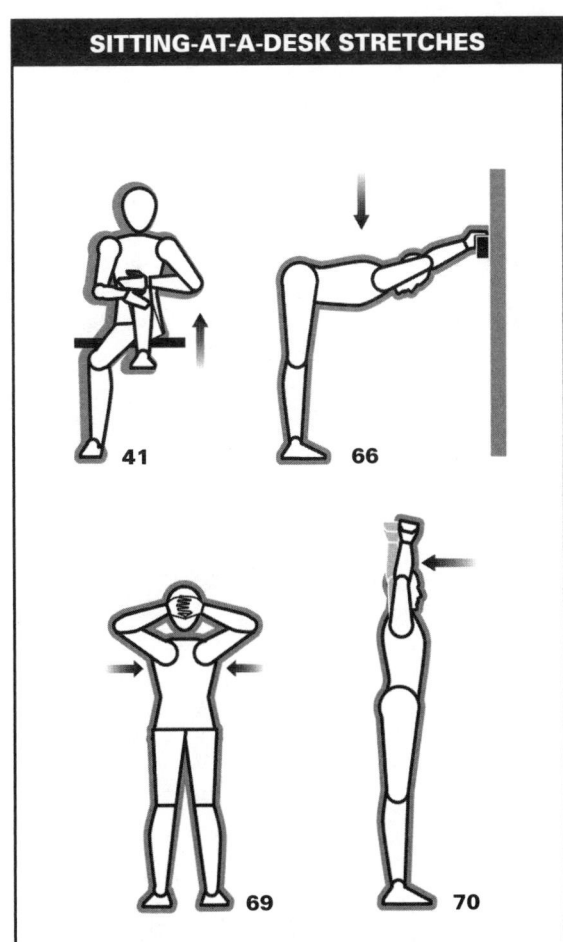

WATCHING TELEVISION STRETCHES

Sorry to disturb your viewing, but there are lots of stretches you can do while watching ball games, movies, and sit-coms on television. Most of them can be executed right there in the recliner, but it probably wouldn't hurt to get up every once in a while to give your back a break. Here are four made-for-TV stretches: Sitting Lower Back #43, Sitting Twist #52, Overhead Shoulder #70, and Sit Back, Lean Back #75 (or Sit Forward, Lean Forward #76).

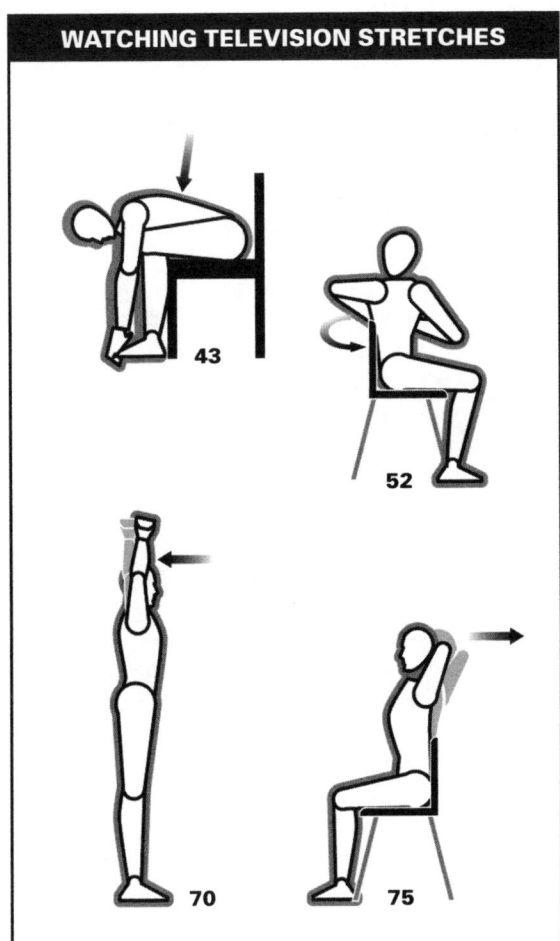

CAR/PLANE STRETCHES

There are not many options for automobile drivers, but car passengers and air travelers confined to small spaces for several hours do have choices. If you are driving or riding in a car, stop at rest areas at least every hour to get out, move around, and perhaps do some of the standing stretches already described and illustrated. Air passengers, try to book an aisle seat, take a break, and walk up and down the aisle for a few minutes. Better yet, ask for an exit-row seat when you check in. The extra leg room will allow more space for lower body stretches.

Assuming you are in a seated position, you may be able to manage Stretches #1, #2, #3, and #4—all for the feet and ankles. How you are dressed and where you are seated may determine which stretches will work on a plane. If you are wearing a skirt or crammed into a center seat, the choices are pretty limited. In the best-case scenario, consider these four stretches: Sitting Twist #52, Shoulder Squeeze #69 (or Overhead Shoulder #70), Forward Shoulder #72, and Side-to-Side Neck #79.

CAR/PLANE STRETCHES

BAD BACK STRETCHES

As much as 80 percent of the general population will suffer from low back pain at some time during their lives. The New England Journal of Medicine reports that, within six weeks, 90 percent of back pain problems resolve themselves with or without treatment. But waiting six weeks when your back is killing you is too much to ask. Here are four stretches described in Chapter 5 for avoiding low back pain and for dealing with it once it develops: Lying Knees-to-Chest #39 (or Sitting Knee-to-Chest #41), Full Body #42, Modified Pushup #48 (or Elbow Prop #49), and Sitting Twist #52 (or Standing Twist #53). In addition, consider some of the hamstring stretches discussed in Chapter 4. Tight hamstrings are often associated with low back pain.

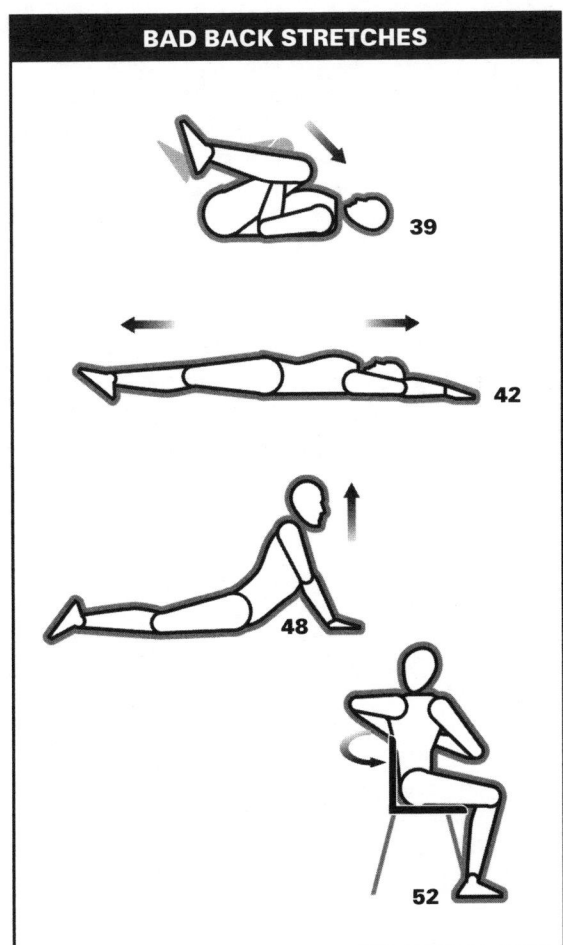

BAD BACK STRETCHES

39

42

48

52

SORE SHOULDERS/NECK STRETCHES

There are several recommended stretches in Chapter 6 for relieving the tension and pain that can easily develop in the neck and shoulders. Most of them can be done sitting or standing, and they can be done at home, at work, in a gym, or in a car. Start with these four from Chapter 5 and occasionally add or substitute others to provide variety in your program and to stretch other upper body areas: Doorway Turn #67 (or Doorway Shoulder #71), Overhead Shoulder #70, Forward Shoulder #72, and any of the neck stretches from #77 to #81. Side-to-Side Neck #79 is illustrated at right.

SORE SHOULDERS/NECK STRETCHES

67

70

72

79

STIFF KNEES STRETCHES

Age, overuse, injury, and the absence of an exercise program can all result in stiff, achy, and noisy knees. Don't worry about the snap, crackle, and pop noises unless they are accompanied by pain. Do something about the pain, stiffness, and limited range of motion, however, before those conditions get worse. The joint itself may be damaged and require aggressive medical treatment, so consult with an orthopedic surgeon before starting a program. Otherwise, carefully stretching the muscles, tendons, and ligaments that support the knee joint can go a long way toward solving some of the problems. Here are four stretches from Chapter 4 that will increase range of motion in the knee joints: Lunge #18, Prone Hamstring #21, Table Top Hamstring #25, and Quadriceps Stork Stand #33.

STIFF KNEES STRETCHES

CHAPTER 10

Twenty Questions

1. Does stretching reduce injuries?
Perhaps indirectly, but the evidence is not conclusive.

2. Can stretching enhance performance? Yes.

3. Does stretching increase a joint's range of motion?
Yes.

4. What is the difference between static and ballistic stretching?
Static stretches are held at the point of resistance. Ballistic stretches involve bouncing at the point of resistance and repeating the stretch without stopping. Most of the stretches in this book are static.

5. What is dynamic stretching?
It is stretching muscles with controlled movements—the kind you would see, for example, in athletes going through the motions of swinging a bat, golf club, or tennis racket.

6. Which type of stretching is safest?
Static.

7. What is PNF stretching?
PNF refers to proprioceptive neuromuscular facilitation, which involves alternating contractions and relaxation movements supervised by a trainer or therapist.

8. How long should you hold a stretch?
In most cases, either 30 seconds or three ten-second holds.

9. How many times should the same stretch be performed during one session?
Two or three times if the stretch is held for less than 30 seconds, but each person should decide how long to hold a stretch for his or her situation.

10. Is there any benefit in holding a stretch longer than 30 seconds? No.

11. How often should you stretch?
Every day, but occasionally missing a day
or weekend is okay.

12. Is it possible to gain strength by stretching?
It's possible for people who are not well
conditioned, but a resistance training program
is usually best for getting stronger.

13. What is the stretch reflex? It's when a muscle
is stretched to an extreme. At that point, a nerve
impulse signals the muscle to contract. The
stretch reflex protects muscles from tearing.

**14. Should you stretch before *and* after a workout
or event?** Yes.

15. Why stretch afterward?
Because the temperature of muscle tissue
is warmer, making it easier to stretch.

**16. Should you stretch first or warm up, and then
stretch?** Warm up first, then stretch.

17. Is it possible to hurt yourself stretching?
Yes, but it's not likely to happen if you choose
the correct stretches and execute them properly.

18. Does flexibility diminish with age?
Yes, unless you do something about it.

19. Is it possible to be too flexible?
Yes. Some people are so flexible that their joints are not stable.

20. Are there age restrictions regarding stretching?
People of any age can (and should) stretch, but the types, intensity, and frequency of stretches might vary with age.

INDEX